REVENGE

REVENGE

A Short Enquiry into Retribution

STEPHEN FINEMAN

REAKTION BOOKS

Published by Reaktion Books Ltd
Unit 32, Waterside
44–48 Wharf Road
London N1 7UX, UK
www.reaktionbooks.co.uk

First published 2017
Copyright © Stephen Fineman 2017

Printed and bound in Great Britain by
TJ International, Padstow, Cornwall

A catalogue record for this book is available from the British Library

ISBN 978 1 78023 840 1

CONTENTS

PREFACE

Where would we be without revenge? 'All the better', many would say. Yet as social animals, our compulsion to avenge a wrongdoing is among the most primal of human urges, and not without reason. It deals with threats to one's well-being, territory, pride, honour, esteem, identity or role. Getting even shows there is a price to pay for wrongdoing. It resets the equilibrium and pecking order, a tacit rule of feuding couples, aggrieved workers, conflicting tribes or warring nations. It is the ultimate statement of self and community, both a protective and a warning to others to keep away – justice in the raw.

So we are all avengers at heart, but our heads tell us differently. We are taught that revenge should be suppressed, diverted or dealt with by 'the authorities'. There are justice systems intended to limit revenge and stop it spiralling out of control (although they can make matters worse when justice depends on how wealthy you are, or on your colour, race or gender). Religion adds its contentious voice. The core texts of the Abrahamic religions envisage a world where love, compassion, turning the other cheek and forgiveness prevail, and where revenge should rarely surface. But religious authority is assuredly malleable, often twisted to suit the giver's or receiver's needs. Sceptics note that turning the other cheek is simply an invitation to be slapped again, while 'righteous revenge' and 'serving God's purpose' are among the most fluid phrases in the religious lexicon. They have been used to justify some of the bloodiest acts of vengeance in human history.

Revenge fascinates. It has long engaged novelists, playwrights and film-makers, and been pored over by philosophers and social scientists. Its potential for destruction makes it a central concern of government. It can be instantaneous or pre-planned – the 'dish served cold' – harnessing the best and worst of human ingenuity. But if we look at revenge with a dispassionate eye, what does it tell us about the 'human condition'? Does revenge always deserve the condemnation associated with it? Is there a crucial tipping point between 'good' and 'bad' revenge? After all, we readily warm to the avenger who rights a wrong by breaking the rules, and we fight wars on the premise of justified revenge. In this book I suggest that revenge is not always the monster it is made out to be, and in many ways we cannot live without it. But there is another side. As revenge morphs into ever more complex and dangerous forms, it has become much harder to manage. What, then, are our options?

When immersed in a subject, authors will often tell you that the world gradually appears to be saturated with examples of what they are researching; they seem to pop up everywhere. Revenge is certainly no exception. As I cast my eye over my daily newspaper, watch the news, read a novel and listen to some of my friends' woes, revenge in some form or other appears. There seems abundant evidence that there is no such thing as a revengeless society.

ONE

THE ROOTS OF REVENGE

Just outside Riyadh, in the caves and crevices of the scorched Saudi Arabian landscape, troops of baboons shelter from the intense sun and survey their terrain. Once very wary of their human neighbours, they have become bolder over time, launching raids on farms and houses in search of food and drink. But what happened in 2000 shifted the goalposts. According to newspaper reports, a local resident was driving along the road from Mecca to Taif and accidentally struck and killed a baboon at the side of the road. He continued on his way, to return along the same stretch of road three days later, totally unprepared for what happened next. A baboon screeched out a cry of recognition when it saw the car, a rally call to the rest of the troop to launch an ambush. They bombarded the car with stones and ripped out its windscreen. Severely shaken, the driver barely managed to escape unscathed.[1]

Resembling a scene from *Planet of the Apes,* this event is hard to credit. However, it depicts what primatologists dub a 'revenge system' common to our primate ancestors. In truth, we can only guess what the baboons might have felt when they lost a member of their community, or whether the urge for revenge was actually on their minds before the car was spotted. However, as not too distant relatives of ours, their actions bear all the hallmarks of human revenge.

Detailed studies of the social life of primates, particularly chimpanzees and macaques, reveal their excellent memories. They can recall who offended them and will postpone retaliation until a suitable opportunity arises. Reciprocity regulates a chimpanzee's daily life, not only in returning blows but in sharing food with those who have previously shared their food with them. Struggles for power, rank and hierarchy are enforced by dominant group members who freely inflict punishment, usually beatings, on rule breakers.[2] At the top of the pyramid alpha males enjoy their privileges: the safest sleeping places, the best food and the most desirable females. Revenge is swift on usurpers. Certainly, any chimp who acts above its station has to contend with the pain of decisive retribution. Strangers are not welcome: rhesus macaques will attack their own image in a mirror, believing a stranger is threatening them. Male chimps regularly patrol their community boundaries and, should they happen upon members of a neighbouring community, they will attack, often brutally. Occasionally the social order is upturned when an alliance of subordinate families attack and overthrow the dominant family: a coup d'état. By deterring freeloaders and penalizing rule breakers, the species has gained ascendancy over their socially fragmented competitors.

And so it is with the human primate. Revenge is a persistent and powerful human drive, fixed in our biosocial make-up and triggered by strong emotions: sorrow, grief, humiliation, anger or rage. As far as we can tell, prehistoric bands of roving hunter-gatherers generally enjoyed each other's company, sharing their resources. Disputes over meat cheating or bullying could be resolved by distancing or expelling an offender. But more severe threats to the tribe, such as killings or kidnappings of females, demanded harsher justice: revenge killings by high-status males.

Struggles for dominance and best mating, if successful, gave evolutionary advantage to the tribe by reinforcing the resilience of the group.

Matters became more complex when tribes became attached to the land and groups grew in size. The importance of protecting kinships and status intensified and different feuding patterns evolved: chains of reprisal to protect property and self-esteem, with rules about who could take whose life, when and where. The complex cultural shaping of revenge had begun. As societies began to sprawl and urbanize, revenge's main drawbacks came to the fore: it was anarchic and uncontrolled. The state would now do the job that revenge had done, but impartially and dispassionately, backed by anti-revenge teaching. In taking revenge, declared Francis Bacon, 'a man is but even with his enemy, but in passing it over he is superior', while Catholic canon law regarded the very contemplation of revenge as a venial sin. Poets and philosophers added their voices: 'Before you embark on a journey of revenge, dig two graves,' said Confucius. 'Revenge, at first thought sweet, Bitter ere long, back on itself recoils,' opined Milton.

It would seem that there is not much to be said for revenge; but maybe that tips the baby out with the bathwater. Negotiating relationships can involve minor tit-for-tats of the sort that do not merit the moralist's condemnation or the concerns of the law. Revenge cannot replace what is lost, such as property, a family member or a friend, but it can restore attendant losses such as pride and honour. In these circumstances it is rational to seek revenge, as Friedrich Nietzsche notes: 'If our honour has suffered through our adversary, revenge can restore it . . . By revenge we prove that we are not afraid of him either, and herein lies the settlement, the readjustment.'[3] Third-party retaliation cannot do this, which is why duels persisted well after they were made illegal, and why extrajudicial punishments occur in all societies. When an offender is punished by others it misses the ownership that a victim can crave; the primal immediacy of delivering justice by one's own hand. The fact that it can trigger counter-revenge is of little concern to the avenger; 'he very often cold-bloodedly anticipates it', says Nietzsche. The compelling objective is the other's suffering, regardless.

Revenge may be frowned upon, but that does not prevent people wanting or imagining it. Victims of rape, mugging, violent robbery or atrocities will often report long-term revenge fantasies. A study of Kosovar Albanians after the end of the war in Kosovo found that half of the men and a little under half of the women reported desires for revenge against perpetrators in the first few months, and a year later little had changed.[4] Likewise, combat troops suffering post-traumatic stress describe their survival guilt and persisting fantasies about avenging the loss of their close buddies. But murderous thoughts about revenge are not confined to physical traumas; any profound humiliation or betrayal can be reason enough. Jon Ronson cites the office worker who imagined 'tampering with my boss's car brakes so he'd have a braking failure on the motorway', because the boss had mocked him in front of other people.[5] A jilted woman tells of her reactions towards the man she had loved so passionately, letting 'revenge fantasies fill the whole of her interior self':

> I imagined that my lover would be involved in some terrible accident – and that as a result he would be a paraplegic; he would have no use of his legs – maybe even he would have no legs. But – here is the kicker – his mind would be totally intact. And, in this state, he would finally come to realize that I truly loved him, that my love was

the most valuable thing that he had ever had in his life – and that without my love, he was doomed to live out his last awful years, with no love.[6]

Revenge fantasies are coping mechanisms, the second best to actual revenge. If we cannot actually damage or destroy an adversary, we can do it in our head, and maybe feel a little better for it.

FOR SOME people, violent revenge and vindictiveness are default reactions when they feel threatened or under stress. Extreme reactions of this sort are often rooted in early life experiences, particularly with over-controlling, sadistic parental figures. The child learns to mirror their parents' behaviour, masking their own feelings of anxiety and inferiority with ego-boosting defences. In time these convert into a longing to triumph over their adversaries: the power to exploit others is thrilling and self-affirming, a predilection that has been labelled 'malignant narcissism'.[7]

Narcissism can be viewed as a spectrum: healthy at one end, malignant at the other. Psychoanalyst Heinz Kohut describes malignant narcissism as 'one of the most pernicious afflictions of the human psyche . . . acted out, in disconnected vengeful acts or in a cunningly plotted vendetta'.[8] Malignant narcissists are typically obsessively vain and treat others as relatively worthless and exploitable. They project an inflated self-importance or grandiosity, fantasizing about power and unimpeded success, and are quick to rage. They can be found in all walks of life: the petty tyrant in the office, factory or school; the obsessively vengeful partner or lover. Some disguise this side of their character behind a facade of bonhomie or charm. In the workplace they may exude a single-mindedness and sense of purpose associated with good leadership, but the flipside is their ruthlessness and manipulativeness. Working for such a boss can be painful, as one victim explains: 'Over two years, this arsehole drove me to the brink of suicide, deep depression, and totalled my self-esteem. All the while managing to somehow manipulate me into believing it was my entire fault.'[9]

Given the right conditions some malignant narcissists rise to positions of extraordinary power. James Fallon, Professor of Psychiatry at the University of California, sees them as genuine psychopaths: charming, charismatic and intelligent, but also 'extremely self-absorbed, masterful liars, compassionless, often sadistic, and possess a boundless appetite for power'.[10] The long list includes Hitler, Mussolini, Stalin, Mao Tse-tung, Idi Amin, Kim Jong-il, Pol Pot, Saddam Hussein and Muammar Gaddafi. Hitler's persona-switching has been well documented; he was praised by his secretary for his 'gentle, flattering tone'. Saddam Hussein was known to display an engaging sense of humour, and Stalin, by repute, could be 'irresistibly amiable'.[11] The lives of these despots have been scrutinized in considerable detail, revealing how malignant narcissism can evolve into a grotesquely destructive force. Stalin and Saddam Hussein are chilling examples.

Stalin's turbulent childhood truly shaped the man. His father was an alcoholic and physically abused him and his mother. His mother, emotionally distant and illiterate, wanted her son to become a priest, so installed him in a seminary where the beatings continued, but now at the hands of the priests.[12] He was expelled for his hostility towards his teachers and his penchant for Karl Marx over the Bible.

Stalin became alienated from his parents, aggravated by stigmatizing rumours about his illegitimacy. One candidate for his biological father was his godfather, Koba Egnatashvili, a wrestling champion and wealthy merchant. Stalin came to idealize him, so much so that he took his name, Koba, when he became a revolutionary. Nevertheless, he struggled with his sense of inferiority and his physical appearance – badly scarred from smallpox, a half-paralysed arm and twisted gait. He compensated by inflating his self-esteem and shutting down emotionally, especially after the death from typhus of his first wife, Kato. Emotional numbness and lack of empathy meant he would readily resort to brutality to achieve his ends. For a period in his youth he organized armed robberies, including cold-blooded killings, but when he came to power he erased this part of his past by executing his previous gang members. Dealing in fear and death came easy to him, fuelled by a growing paranoia after the Great Terror of 1936. His supporters could fall victim to his sudden shifts in mood. Reputedly, he signed tens of thousands of death warrants in a single day, then calmly sat back to watch a movie. He presided over an ideological system that normalized cruelty.

Escalating grandiosity, a hallmark of malignant narcissists, camouflaged Stalin's insecurities. He renamed himself at least six times. Born Josef Dzhugashvili, he assumed the name of Stalin after the Russian word for 'steel', then Comrade Stalin, then Great Stalin, then Our Great Leader, and finally Father of the Nation. His self-salutations were bolstered by street portraits, giant statues, buildings, posters and songs, reminding everyone of his magnificence and potency, a predilection of dictators throughout the ages.[13] Adulation from his inner circle was laced with fear. In *The Gulag Archipelago* Aleksandr Solzhenitsyn tells of the fate of a man who made the disastrous mistake of being the first to stop applauding at one of Stalin's conferences:

For three minutes, four minutes, five minutes, the stormy applause, rising to an ovation, continued . . . It was becoming insufferably silly even to those who really adored Stalin . . . The director of the local paper factory, an independent and strong-minded man, stood with the presidium. Aware of all the falsity and all the impossibility of the situation, he still kept on applauding! Nine minutes! Ten! . . . Then, after eleven minutes, the director of the paper factory assumed a business-like expression and sat down in his seat . . . The squirrel had been smart enough to jump off his revolving wheel. That, however, was how they discovered who the independent people were. And that was how they went about eliminating them. That same night the factory director was arrested. They easily pasted ten years on him on the pretext of something quite different.[14]

Behind Stalin's carefully crafted image, costs were mounting. He lost touch with the real dangers around him. Purges of his officer corps weakened and demoralized his military and he scorned warnings about an imminent German invasion. As his health deteriorated his personal doctor advised that he should ease off his duties, to which Stalin flew into a rage and ordered his immediate arrest. All doctors, especially Jewish ones, were now 'murderers in white gowns' out to poison prominent Soviet figures. Stalin died from a massive stroke amid rumours that his security chief, Lavrentiy Beira, had engineered it.

Like Stalin, Saddam Hussein's malignant narcissism was forged in childhood. His father left before he was born and his teenage brother died of cancer, a huge blow to his mother. Depressed and destitute, she had tried to abort Saddam and attempted suicide. The young boy's care was then transferred to his maternal uncle, Khairallah Talfah in Tikrit, but Saddam was returned to his mother after she remarried to a distant relative, an abusive man who took an instant dislike to Saddam, beating and degrading him.

From around ten years old Saddam began to live up to the Arabic meaning of his name – 'one who confronts', or 'powerful collider'. He resented both his stepfather and his mother, especially after they refused to let him have an education. So he abandoned them and returned to the care of Khairallah Talfah. There, his wounded self turned from despair to thoughts of grandeur under the tutorage of his uncle, now his political mentor. Talfah later became Governor of Baghdad, a fervent nationalist with a hatred of foreigners. His credentials were cogently articulated in a pamphlet he wrote in 1940, *Three Whom God Should Not Have Created: Persians, Jews, and Flies*, widely circulated by Saddam when he came to power. Talfah helped enrol Saddam into a nationalistic school in Baghdad where Saddam was teased about his late start and poor literacy, but it was his teachers' stiff discipline and corporal punishment that offended him most. According to his biographer, Shiva Balaghi, he once slipped a snake into a teacher's robe under the subterfuge of an embrace, and also tried to kill a teacher.[15]

Thanks to his uncle, the impressionable young Saddam absorbed the militaristic xenophobia that promised to rescue Iraq from imperial powers. Saddam's dreams of grandeur were now beginning to gel, dispelling the self-doubts of his early years. Admired by Ba'ath party officials for his thuggishness in their service, he rose rapidly through the ranks, exploiting rivalries in the party to bring it, and himself, to power in Iraq. There are many examples of Saddam's volatility and ruthlessness. In a meeting convened to address Iraq's setbacks in its war with Iran, Saddam asked his ministers for their candid advice on the way forward. The minister of health suggested that Saddam temporarily step down and resume the presidency after peace had been established. Saddam reportedly thanked him for his candour and ordered his arrest. The minister's wife pleaded for her husband's return and Saddam reassured her that it would happen. The next day his body was sent to her in a canvas bag, chopped into pieces.[16]

This brutal incident was upstaged by the grotesque 'traitors meeting' of 18 July 1979. Some four hundred people were assembled in a large conference hall. Dressed in military uniform, Saddam strode slowly up to the lectern flourishing a cigar and announced, sad-faced and wearily, the existence of a counter-revolutionary plot to overthrow him and the party. There were traitors present, he said, but everyone would have an opportunity to make up their own minds. The atmosphere froze. He sat down puffing on his cigar, and the secretary general of the Command Council was ushered into the room from behind a curtain. He was smartly dressed, but plainly a broken man. From a rehearsed script he confessed his role in the plot and declared specific details, dates and meetings. He then named the traitors in the room. The fear was miasmatic. As each name was called out a security official in plain clothes grabbed the man and led him out of the hall. In panic, some people rose to their feet to loudly proclaim their fealty to their leader, 'Glory to Saddam Hussein our leader, all praise to him!' Saddam looked on impassively, drawing steadily on his cigar.[17]

Sixty 'traitors' were taken from the room, leaving the rest of the audience in little doubt about the shape of things to come under Saddam's rule. Saddam returned to the lectern teary-eyed to repeat the names of those who had betrayed him. Others, doubtless massively relieved, mimicked his tearfulness. As

Saddam's mood lightened, so did theirs. The meeting closed on a surreal note of cheers, clapping and laughter, an approval that clearly pleased Saddam. But his master stroke was yet to come. He put a gun into the hand of each surviving member of the party's inner circle and ordered them personally to shoot the condemned men – in the basement of the building where the plot was said to be hatched. It was a move that welded them absolutely to his power.[18]

The history of leadership points to the paradox of malignant narcissism. On the one hand it attracts certain followers, drawn to the leader's prejudices, uncompromising style and charisma – promises of good times ahead. On the other hand, the leader's growing paranoia and vindictiveness eventually ensures his own destruction, along with many around them.

TWO

RELIGIOUS VOICES

The world's great religions – Judaism, Christianity, Islam, Buddhism and Hinduism – have been central in moralizing revenge and, in the main, condemning it. Insofar as there is a general message, it is: the world is replete with insults, suffering and pain, a reality of human existence, but man's revenge only makes matters worse. Justice is not a free-for-all. This does not mean that revenge cannot be justified, but that is a decision for the deities and their earthly agents. God always avenges from pure motives; man does not.

But this message is presented in different ways, depending on the religious authority. The rabbinic authors of the Talmud were well attuned to the downsides of personal revenge. The Talmud embraces the sacred five books of Moses and the Jewish oral traditions, and is the source of Jewish law. It warns against the destructive force of anger, rage and vengeance and praises those who are unjustly treated but manage to resist the temptation to avenge. 'Anger', according to Rabbi Simeon Lakish, 'deprives the sage of his wisdom, a prophet of his vision'.[1] God tells Moses to 'not seek revenge or bear a grudge against anyone among your people, but love your neighbour as yourself. I am the Lord' (Leviticus 19:18). Those who challenge God's omnipotence and mislead his people, however, are not spared: God entreats the

Israelites to join him in his revenge against the Midianites, a nomadic race of idolaters who led Israel astray in worshipping different gods (Numbers 31:2). And in Deuteronomy, God's wrath is made crystal clear: 'It is mine to avenge; I will repay. In due time their foot will slip; their day of disaster is near and their doom rushes upon them' (32:35).

Jewish sages are divided on whether Judaic prohibitions on taking revenge apply to all situations. For example, the Talmud forbids revenge against someone who refuses to lend money, but it is less clear about those who cause emotional pain. There is leniency when vengeance is motivated by genuine altruism to enlighten an offending party, a decidedly slippery notion to prove. In terms of daily justice, Exodus reveals a compendium of laws, many of them remarkable for their humanity and fair mindedness. They cover a wide range of transgressions and disputes: the treatment of servants, murder, manslaughter, violent assault, theft, rape, idolatry, treatment of disadvantaged people, money and property, lending, justice and equal standing before the law. Compassion and compensation appear overriding concerns, except when physical injury is deliberately inflicted. Murderers are put to death, and thereafter it is an 'eye for an eye, tooth for a tooth, hand for a hand, foot for foot, burning for burning, wound for wound, stripe for stripe' (Exodus 21:24–5), a seemingly barbaric set of laws. But some religious scholars have concluded that this verse was never intended to be taken literally in Jewish law, and rarely was; it was regarded as a trope for deciding appropriate damages and compensation for an injury – often monetary.[2]

CHRISTIANITY DISTANCES itself decisively from revenge:

> You have heard that it was said, 'Eye for eye, and tooth
> for tooth'. But I tell you, do not resist an evil person. If
> anyone slaps you on the right cheek, turn to them the
> other cheek also. And if anyone wants to sue you and
> take your shirt, hand over your coat as well (Matthew
> 5:38–42).

These were Jesus's exhortations to his disciples and onlookers in
his Sermon on the Mount. He asked people to love their enemies
and pray for those who persecuted them, sentiments reproduced
many times in the New Testament. Pain and loss caused by others
should be left for God to judge, expressed movingly by Jesus on
the cross: 'Father, forgive them, for they know not what they do.'
The very difficulty in forsaking revenge is a major reason why
forgiving is considered so praiseworthy in Christian writings and
integral to the ritual of confession in Catholicism. A Catholic
who wilfully takes revenge is considered a sinner and, if a serious
attack, subject to God's vengeance in Hell – unless they pay God's
price for forgiveness: confession and penances.

Christian theology confronts the futility of revenge in war:
it fans flames of hatred; state terrorism does not bring peace but
despair, so 'Blessed are the peacemakers, for they will be called
children of God' (Matthew 5:9). Yet history reveals Christianity's
confusing loyalties when it sponsors retribution or acquiesces
silently to it. The Crusades, the Inquisition, the justification
of slavery, support for the death penalty and anti-Semitism are
among the infamous examples.[3] In Nazi Germany, Catholic and
Protestant pastors, priests and bishops were prepared to declare
from their pulpits that God had blessed Hitler's cause, and it

was a Christian's duty to join the military and fight and kill for the Führer. In more recent times American-led wars have fired the enthusiasm of evangelical Christians and mainstream church leaders, some of them active supporters of the Bush wars.

ISLAM ACKNOWLEDGES the Old Testament's 'eye for an eye' in its own law of retaliation, or *qisas*. In cases of serious assault or murder, judicial retribution permits the victim or the deceased's representative to demand exactly the same fate for the perpetrator. But there are other options – blood money as compensation or forgiveness: 'whosoever forgives and makes amends, his reward is upon God' (Quran 42:40). Like the Christian and Jewish scriptures, the Quran has passages that advocate peace and others that are warlike. The Prophet Muhammad's default position, however, is mercy and forgiveness, even in the direst circumstances: 'Let them forgive and overlook: do you not wish God to forgive you? For God is oft-forgiving, Most Merciful' (24:22). But Islam cannot be viewed as monolithic, with more than seventy subsects derived from five contrasting branches: Shia, Sunni, Wahhabi, Sufi and Ahmaddiya. Some of them are bitterly divided over the true nature of Islam, and are prepared to wage bloody retribution on the other to defend their position. Wahhabism in particular is vehemently opposed to the Shia branch of Islam.

Muslim life is characterized by jihad, or 'struggle'. There are three kinds: the believer's internal spiritual jihad to be a good Muslim, the jihad to create a virtuous Islamic society and the jihad to defend Islam. Retaliation and punishment can play a greater or lesser part in this struggle, depending on how Quranic injunctions are interpreted. In the face of an attack on Islamic faith or territory, the Quran calls for a holy war, but not without compassion for innocent women, children and the elderly. In practice, the caveat has been largely ignored by Islamic extremists. Following the devastating attacks of 11 September 2001, Osama bin Laden claimed he was acting under 'the guidance of Allah and the blessed fruit of the jihad . . . I was ordered fight the people until they say there is no god but Allah.' The leader of Jaish-e-Mohammed, a Pakistan affiliate of Al-Qaeda, put it even more bluntly: 'We have not launched jihad at the dictation of anybody and we would not stop at anyone's dictation too . . . We do not care whether the world considers us terrorists.'[4] Extreme interpretations of the Quran fuel violent jihadism, a cause of blessed martyrdom to the jihadist fighter, but to their enemies – other Muslims and non-Muslims – sheer terrorism. Fundamentalist Muslims bridle at the West's liberal attitudes towards sex, adultery, single parenthood and homosexuality, and strict interpretations of Sharia law are used to justify harsh reprisal against those who violate Islamic morality laws.

HINDUISM IS one of the oldest of the world's religions, with some 900 million followers, most of them in India. Unlike Judaism, Christianity and Islam, there is no single deity or scripture, but a set of religious texts, the Veda, containing hymns, incantations and rituals. There are four main Hindu sects – Vaishnavism, Saivism, Shaktism and Smartism – each with its favoured gods, but united in the belief in karma and reincarnation. Karma states that the pain caused to others will always rebound negatively on the perpetrator in this life or a future one. We cannot hurt others without getting hurt back: 'Worthless are those who injure others vengefully,' says Thiruvalluvar, an Indian philosopher and Hindu saint, 'those who stoically endure are like stored gold. Just as the Earth bears those who dig into her, it is best to bear with those who despise us.'

The Hindu doctrine of *ahimsa* enshrines non-retaliation and non-injury. One should refrain from violent words, actions or thoughts about any living thing. As no one is intrinsically evil, another's hurtful behaviour should be met with peace and understanding, not revenge; compassion and empathy are overriding virtues. Hinduism does, however, draw a distinction between revenge and self-defence: force is justified in a self-defensive war, but carefully constrained. Ancient Hindu battle rules state that it is unjust to strike someone from behind, or to poison the tip of an arrow, and it is unforgivable to attack the sick or old, children or women (Rig Veda 1–39:2). A warrior who breaks these rules is condemned to karmic suffering.

Despite Hinduism's inherent passivity, it has been dogged by conflicts with fundamentalist Islam, two systems that could not be further apart. While Hinduism is pantheistic, tolerant of other faiths and not interested in conversion, Islamic fundamentalism is monotheistic, evangelical, intensely doctrinal and historically bent on expansion. Tensions can be traced to the invasion of India by Sultan Mahmud of Ghazni in the year 1000, a bid to enlarge his already extensive Muslim empire in and around Afghanistan. Hindu resistance was meagre and poorly organized, and some 50,000 Hindus lost their lives. It heralded Muslim invasions of the subcontinent well into the eighteenth century, aftershocks that can be felt today in the animosity between Pakistan and India, and in sporadic revenge attacks on minority Hindus in Pakistan, and minority Muslims in India.

MOST OF the world's Buddhist population, estimated to be around 500 million, are concentrated in the Asia-Pacific region. Buddhism is the majority faith in Thailand, Burma (Myanmar), Sri Lanka, Cambodia, Bhutan, Laos and Mongolia. It shares with

Hinduism the notion of karma, but differs in disavowing any personal god or gods, to the extent that some are reluctant to call it a religion. Over 2,000 years Buddhism has divided into different sects that follow their own liturgies, rituals and canons, such as Zen, Pure, Land, Nichiren and Vajrayana. There are doctrinal disagreements, but all follow the teachings of Buddha.

A clue to Buddhism's spiritual tradition lies in its name, a derivation of *budh* meaning 'awakened' or 'enlightened'. The Buddha was the title given some 2,500 years ago to Siddhartha Gautama, a man of royalty and privilege in Nepal. The story goes that he was taken aback to discover the foetid poverty and deprivation beyond his palace gates. In humility, he experimented with a more frugal lifestyle of deep contemplation. It was to become the bedrock of Buddhist practice, a route to nirvana, a state of ultimate enlightenment and 'right mindfulness'. Rage, anger and the desire for revenge are, for Buddhists, a personal responsibility and not to be projected onto others. Thus vengeance is a failure to recognize that the enemy is not the other person, but resides within oneself, as the Buddha says:

If anyone were to give you a blow with the hand, or hit you with a clod of earth, or with a stick, or with a sword, even then you should abandon those urges and thoughts which are worldly [and] you should train yourself thus: 'Neither shall my mind be affected by this, nor shall I give vent to evil words; but I shall remain full of concern and pity, with a mind of love, and I shall not give in to hatred.'[5]

Some Buddhists do not rule out the possibility of revenge that prevents future harm but, akin to the Talmudic altruistic revenge, it has to be free from hatred.

As with other religions, earthly politics distort some of Buddhism's spiritual ideals. There are militaristic sects in Buddhism, a perplexing position for a faith committed to the very opposite. Following years of civil war in Sri Lanka, firebrand Buddhist monks have resisted appeasement with minority 'outsiders' – Tamil Hindus and Muslims, whose homes and shops have been destroyed in vengeance attacks. Burma has witnessed similar violence, where traditionally moderate Rohingya Muslims are now one of the most persecuted groups in the world, on the receiving end of violent racist attacks. At the forefront of their persecution are Buddhist nationalists, whose spiritual leader, Ashin Wirathu, has asserted: 'You can be full of kindness and love, but you cannot sleep next to a mad dog.'[6]

RELIGION AND revenge intertwine, thus attempts to manage revenge inevitably intersect with religious belief and dogma. As we have seen, even for the pious, anti-revenge scriptures can be tough to live up to and readily twisted to suit the believer's politics and passions. It is, of course, profoundly ironic that religious doctrine has so often been hijacked to justify appalling acts of vengeance on one's fellow human beings. When we talk about suppressing or civilizing revenge, religion remains, at best, a very mixed blessing.

THREE

WRITING REVENGE

I f fiction is the 'lie through which we tell the truth', as Albert Camus wrote, then it can tell us a lot of truths about revenge. It can capture revenge's primal hold on our imagination. We can freely immerse ourselves in tales of pain, misfortune and evil, and thrill as the heroic protagonist (our wishful self) delivers retribution to a wrongdoer. In well-crafted stories we can align ourselves variously with the victim, the perpetrator or the detached onlooker.[1]

Revenge has been a staple of romance and crime fiction for centuries, appearing in literature dating back to Sophocles and Shakespeare. More than 1,900 years ago the Roman philosopher and statesman Lucius Annaeus Seneca adapted Greek myths about the abhorrence of revenge. Many of his characters were grisly avengers, like Atreus in *Thyestes*. Atreus' bitter rivalry with his twin brother Thyestes over the Mycenaean throne drove him to seduce Thyestes' wife, murder his children and then trick Thyestes into consuming a gruesome soup concocted from his own children's remains. By the end of the play Atreus appears to have escaped scot-free for his crimes, but not so: Thyestes swears vengeance. Seneca's own chequered career played no small part in his writings. He served at Nero's court and profited grandly from Nero's profligacy and crimes (Nero murdered his mother and first wife). Over time, though, Seneca became troubled by his complicity in Nero's regime, but was fearful of speaking out. So he disguised his concerns in his writings. In a coda worthy of one of his own revenge tragedies, Seneca was forced by Nero to take his own life after being accused (possibly falsely) of plotting to kill him. Seneca's writings inspired the revenge tragedies of Renaissance dramatists such as Thomas Kyd and William Shakespeare.

Revenge tragedies are tragic because they end up consuming the righteous avenger and, often, innocent bystanders. Avengers prototypically face a heinous crime that no official agency – the law, the monarch – is willing or able to punish. They yearn for justice and finally take matters into their own hands, but with cataclysmic consequences. The thirteenth-century Icelandic *Njals* and *Volsunga* sagas are remarkable depictions of this theme, believed to have inspired Tolkien's *Lord of the Ring*s. They reveal an ancient Icelandic culture of manhood, honour and superstition, defended by blood feuds that blight families for generations.

The sex, fury and violence of Renaissance revenge tragedies excited contemporary audiences, depicting abuses of power that mirrored the real word. In Thomas Kyd's *The Spanish Tragedy*, Bel-imperia and Hieronimo seek justice for Horatio, Hieronimo's son, who has been murdered by the son of the Portuguese viceroy, egged on by Bel-imperia's brother. Failing to get the law to act, Bel-imperia and Hieronimo kill the two conspirators and then themselves. In Shakespeare's *Hamlet*, Hamlet is visited by the ghost of his father, informing him that he has been murdered by Hamlet's uncle, Claudius. Driven by hate and fury, Hamlet plots revenge. He runs Claudius through with a poisoned sword and forces him to drink poisoned wine. Other members of the court get fatally caught up in the plot and Hamlet himself dies from poisoning. The kingdom is left shattered.

The spirit world is ever present in these works. The Fates wreaked revenge on human folly, making up for puny human justice. Ghosts reminded protagonists and audiences that past transgressions were never forgotten and their injustices would come back to literally haunt them. Shakespeare worked creatively with these themes, recognizing that his audience would have an instinctive sympathy for tit-for-tat revenge. He delivered it in good measure, but not unproblematically. Lethal avengers may be righteous in responding to a cruel or unwarranted death, but in doing so they also became killers. Does one death deserve another in the name of justice? Is doing harm justified to undo harm? Shakespeare often blurs the moral boundaries by portraying malevolent characters as failing and fragile rather than inherently evil, and stressing the conditions that enhance the moral authority of avengers.

The avenging hero is a trope that crosses different media and cultures. In the movie world, for example, we have kung-fu revenge tales, such as Chang Cheh's stylish *One-armed Swordsman* (1967) and *Daredevils of Kung Fu* (1979). The Chinese director King Hu created the first female kung-fu heroine in *Come Drink with Me* (1966). Japanese film-makers have mined their own ancient heritage of Samurai honour, such as Akira Kurosawa's *Seven Samurai* (1954) and *Throne of Blood* (1957), his atmospheric adaption of Shakespeare's *Macbeth*, where we are transported to a ghostly, fog-enshrouded, landscape in feudal Japan. Bollywood, too, has taken to revenge in a big way in Hindi and English-language movies: 'righteous revenge' is delivered to victims of murder, rape, swindling, corruption and human trafficking, reflecting some of the subcontinent's prevalent social concerns.

Aakhree Raasta (1986), for instance, is the story of a wife who commits suicide after being raped by a powerful official, and her husband who is falsely imprisoned for her supposed murder. After 24 years in prison he vows to hunt down those who framed him. The film was a massive box-office hit.

Heroic revenge occupies an iconic position in American popular culture. Laws may be essential, but they jar with America's strong frontier mentality. The Western was cast firmly in this mould, transforming the feudal duel into a modern revenge motif: trial-by-gun in the Wild West. In its crudest form, valiant soldiers, a few dedicated lawmen or right-thinking cowhands are pitted against malevolent, 'primitive' Native Americans or evil bandits. The goodies are invariably white, like well-groomed Roy Rogers, 'king of the cowboys'. With the assistance of his faithful palomino horse, Trigger, he always got his man. He could also turn a good tune or two. These idealized heroes caricatured a settler's view of justice in a hostile landscape – an individual's right to defend their property or family with force. Clint Eastwood's character in *Unforgiven* (1992) caught the tempo. In an iconic scene an artless gunslinger ponders two murdered cowboys: 'Well, I guess they had it commin'.' The Eastwood character is brief in his reply: 'We all got it commin', kid.'

There was a lot of revenge to go around in cinema's Wild West, and things did not always go to plan. In *The Bravados* (1958), for example, rancher Jim Douglas doggedly hunts down and kills three outlaws in revenge for the murder of his wife. But he is then mortified to discover that they were in fact innocent; the real perpetrator was a neighbour who wanted his life savings. He is now no better than a cold-blooded murderer himself. Moral uncertainties also come through John Ford's classic film *The Searchers* (1956). A Comanche raid destroys Ethan Edwards's homestead and kills his wife. The raiders also abduct two of his nieces, raping and murdering one of them. Edwards is a brooding ex-soldier and racist, now obsessed with revenge. Some years pass before he discovers his other niece is alive, but living willingly with the Comanches. This is insufferable for Edwards. In an epic showdown Edwards gets his revenge on the Comanches, killing and scalping the chief. But there is no joy in purpose fulfilled. In the final scene he walks away forlornly from his homestead, destined ever to wander.

'Get ready to root for the bad guy' was the slogan for the 1999 film *Payback*. It abandoned the 'white knight', selfless male hero in favour of a psychologically blemished protagonist who did immoral things for moral reasons: the ends justified the means. Anti-heroes are appealing because, like most of us, they are flawed characters and can speak to our shortcomings as well as our strengths. *Payback*'s anti-hero, Porter, is no saint, and he would not bother anyone unless they bothered him; but then he becomes a force to be reckoned with. We gradually warm to him as he takes revenge against the even badder guys who have cheated him.

Anti-heroes are typically contemptuous of mainstream justice and its obvious failures; for them, there is no choice but to do it themselves, like Harry Callahan in *Dirty Harry* (1971). He is a serving police officer who cares little for the protocols of his police department when it comes to tracking down fellow cops on the make, sick killers or terrorists. He shocks the establishment with his violence, a frontiersman in modern society. He is out of place and out of time – but nevertheless easy to empathize with as he dispenses his personal brand of justice. We can feel similarly about Paul Kersey in Michael Winner's *Death Wish* (1974). During a break-in at his apartment his daughter is raped and his wife is savagely beaten; she subsequently dies. He is traumatized and despairs at the ineffectual police response. Distraught, he takes to walking alone at night in a bleak, crime-ridden New York and vents his frustration in violent attacks on muggers. Shocked at first by what he has done, he gradually slips into a vigilante role, regularly despatching street villains. The police finally catch up with him, but because of the positive public reaction to the fall in crime, they offer him a deal: get out of town, stay out of town and we'll forget this. He decamps to Chicago, where he notices that there is more cleaning-up to do.

Anti-heroes occupy a liminal zone between good and evil. When can doing bad be good? Popular television series such as *Breaking Bad*, *Lost*, *Sons of Anarchy* and *Dexter* probe this terrain. In *Dexter*, Dexter Morgan works as a laboratory assistant in a police department analysing bloodstains. On the surface he appears a normal, responsible man, but his background tells a different story. He is the orphan of a brutally murdered mother and harbours murderous psychopathic tendencies. His adopted father, a policeman, has taught him to channel his killing urge to 'good' purpose: slaying abhorrent criminals, such as mob assassins, rapists and serial killers and Dexter accomplishes this with ruthless skill. His victims are so repellent that we soon begin to sympathize with his deviant mission.

SUPERHEROES ARE the Greek gods of the modern age: indestructible, protecting the innocent from criminals, terrorists, mad scientists and malevolent politicians. They are the 'best' type of avenger, there to help out when all else (the law, policing) fails and, what is more, they are remarkably free of malice. Fired by moral rectitude and extraordinary powers, they embody moral character and sacrifice, qualities in short supply among mere mortals. These wondrous creations – Superman, Spiderman, Iron Man, Batman, Captain America – are awe-inspiring models for coping with adversity. They know just how much retaliatory force is necessary, and when to stop. But do we?[2]

Superheroes never grow old, but they do adapt to the times. In the 1930s Superman landed on Earth from Krypton just as the storm clouds of the Second World War were gathering. Marvel comics recruited him and his stablemate, Captain America, to help the war effort in avenging the attack on Pearl Harbor. They embodied fine American values in the face of a loathsome, sub-human enemy. The front page of a 1941 edition of *Superman* comic portrayed a squirming Hitler and Japanese commander in Superman's iron grip, a rallying image for the American people. In the immediate aftermath of 9/11 Captain America and Spiderman sprang into action once again, helping survivors at Ground Zero. But now they were less sure about the wisdom of revenge, or indeed who precisely were their targets. The message was that even superheroes can have their down moments.[3] A few years later we find Batman struggling with himself in the *Dark Knight* trilogy (2005–12), written in a period of much political turmoil and fears about security. He witnessed the disintegration of his Gotham City as it became a cesspool of corruption, violence and retribution. He had his work cut out, but managed, just, to save Gotham from destruction by a mega bomb. A parable for our time perhaps.

There are superheroes and superheroines. Batgirl, Elektra, Ms Marvel, Supergirl and Wonder Woman have dealt deftly with society's rogues, no less effectively than their male counterparts, with whom they have occasionally collaborated. Over her seventy non-ageing years, Wonder Woman has achieved iconic status in American popular culture, being reinvented many times.[4] Strong and capable, she has battled with male and female villains who go by disturbing names such as Angle Man, Baroness von Gunther, Doctor Psycho and Doctor Poison. In 2016 she was, controversially, rewarded for her efforts by the UN, appointed as 'honorary ambassador for the empowerment of women and girls'.[5] There have been other fictional characters appointed by the UN, such as Winnie the Pooh and Tinkerbell, but Wonder Woman was the first to be presented as an icon of gender equality and justice. Not everyone agreed, arguing that 'a large breasted, white woman of impossible proportions, scantily clad', was hardly the best choice.[6]

The very notion of a powerful female avenger would have appeared daring, even outrageous, in medieval and early modern fiction. It flew in the face of the prevalent patriarchy and women's roles as submissive and nurturing. Aristotle set the misogynistic tone in his *Poetics*: women were 'deformed males', 'unscrupulously clever' and no fit subject for drama, a viewpoint that influenced writers well into the Middle Ages.[7] Homer's and Hesiod's women were hardly noted for their spontaneous deeds or accomplishments, but as satisfiers of male needs: marriageability, childbearing capacity and domesticity. Non-earthly women, though, were construed differently, a foretaste of superheroines to come. Athena in the *Odyssey* was much admired for her powerful control over men and women, and in the *Iliad* Homer introduces the Furies, fearful female spirits of justice and vengeance. Black-robed and fiery-eyed, they would seek out murderers, especially matricides, and drive them insane.

Shakespeare, however, broke the traditional mould. Many of his women openly defied injustices. They would 'raise their voices', writes Marguerite Tassi, 'exercise their wills, and exact revenge in response to wrongs, often grievous wrongs, committed against family members, friends, and their community'.[8]

They were seldom violent, but deployed 'feminine' weapons, their superior language skills and power to emasculate. They would refuse sexual advances, rumour-monger and goad others into conspiracies.[9] Queen Margaret in *Richard III*, Portia in *The Merchant of Venice*, Cordelia in *King Lear* and Tamora in *Titus Andronicus* were created in this vein. Maria in *Twelfth Night* combines cunning and comedy to get her revenge. She is the unassuming lady-in-waiting to Countess Olivia and shares her lady's frustration with Malvolio, the steward of the household. The clue to Malvolio's character lies in his name, 'ill will' in Italian. He is puritanical, self-centred and self-righteous and regularly conflicts with members of the household. Maria vows to bring him down a peg or two. She hatches a plot to drop a letter in Malvolio's path that could be interpreted as coming from Olivia, declaring her secret love for him. To indicate that he feels the same way, the letter asks that he should go around wearing yellow stockings and crossed garters, smiling superciliously and generally being abusive to all the servants, an entreaty to which he gladly accedes. The trick delights the mocking observers onstage as well as the play's audience. He gets his just desserts for his insufferable behaviour. Perhaps. Shakespeare leaves us with an upset Olivia, worried about the way Malvolio has been treated, 'most notoriously abused', and Malvolio swearing revenge on them all.

Shakespeare's guileful women reappear to confront Sir John Falstaff, a rumbustiously offensive character in *The Merry Wives of Windsor*. Falstaff represented much that was wrong with England at the time, a nation infested with class prejudice, corruption and disease. Falstaff's forte was swindling, taking bribes from able-bodied soldiers and recruiting frail men into military service. He tried to seduce two prominent Windsor ladies, who responded with a labyrinthine plot to expose his duplicity. It resulted in a string of humiliations for the man who was eventually banished in disgrace. In *Henry v* we learn that his still-unredeemed lifestyle of brothels and taverns finally caught up with him: he died unpleasantly from a type of venereal disease. Justice – at all levels?

In different ways, modern movies have challenged the assumption that violent vengeance is the preserve of men. In *Fatal Attraction* (1987), for instance, female violence is equated with psychopathology. Dan, a successful married lawyer, has a steamy weekend fling with Alex, a publishing executive, while his wife and daughter are away for the weekend. He then wants it to end, but Alex is – understandably – upset about being unceremoniously dumped. She clings on, showing all the signs of erotomania. As their interactions become more violent, where she leads the way, she finally ends up as the main casualty and adulterous Dan walks back to his 'happy' marriage. In contrast, François Truffaut's film *The Bride Wore Black* (1968) is fully behind the avenging female. A grief-stricken bride turns cold avenger after a group of men gun down her husband on their wedding day. Aloof and attractive, she lures each to their death – by knife, poison, arrow or suffocation. Quentin Tarantino follows a similar format in his *Kill Bill* (2003–4). Beatrix Kiddo miraculously survives a murderous attack on her wedding party, but loses her unborn child. She then embarks on a journey of icy revenge, despatching her victims, one by one, with her lethal samurai sword.[10]

Rape in early twentieth-century film would often be a prurient spectacle, and little more. Later productions shifted the goalposts. Instead of being defenceless, rape victims would become justified avengers. The rape-revenge genre was born. Plots were typically hard-hitting: a woman was brutally raped; she survived to hunt down and kill her rapist. It was excessive but vindicated revenge. Movies such as *The Accused, I Spit on Your Grave, Ms 45, Irreversible, Lipstick, The Ladies Club, Thriller, The Girl with the Dragon Tattoo* and *Sudden Impact* are of this ilk. The graphic image of the empowered victim was not lost on some women: 'My reactions startled me. As she shot the rapist again and again, I yelled: "Don't stop shooting until there is nothing left of him". My body arched as if I had the gun in my hands, and I acted out that scene.'[11]

Jonathan Kaplan's landmark film *The Accused* (1988) treated rape justice rather differently. Loosely based on a real case in Massachusetts, Sarah Tobias escapes to a sleazy bar after a fight with her drug-dealer boyfriend. She drinks too much, dances provocatively to the jukebox and flirts with a man who is also drunk. Then things get out of hand. He brutally rapes her in the bar while two men hold her down and others cheer them on. She finally struggles free and runs out, crying for help. Thus far the film shocks and leaves the question of culpability hanging. Given her 'dubious' character and behaviour, could she be fairly accused of bringing it on herself? She goes to law for retribution and her attorney decides to play it safe, arguing for a plea bargain in which Sarah receives compensation, but the perpetrators do not have to admit rape. Sarah is furious; she wants a rape conviction, so her lawyer tries a different tack: to go after the 'passive' onlookers. Against the odds she wins; all are found guilty of criminal solicitation, they are complicit bystanders.[12]

THERE IS a sizeable children's literature on revenge, but those looking for a consistent message will be disappointed. Some writers give a clear impression that revenge is wrong and shameful, others that it is often justified and empowering, and still others that it can be either of these and also fun. Arguably, this is a fair primer for the mixed signals about revenge in the adult world.

For instance, the young characters in Marianne Musgrove's *The Beginner's Guide to Revenge* each hold a grudge that demands revenge, or so they think. As they work together on their plans and possibilities, dissect their motives and think about the people affected, revenge gradually emerges as the least ennobling response.[13] In contrast, Francesca Simon's Henry, in *Horrid Henry's Perfect Day*, decides that the best way of getting his own back on his irritatingly perfect brother is to suddenly stop tormenting him and be super-perfect himself. It works a treat. His brother is maddened by Henry's change in behaviour and throws a tantrum (as well as a plate), which gets him confined to his bedroom. It delights Henry – revenge is both sweet and fun.[14] Charles in *Diary of a Mean Teacher*, by M. P. Rolland, has a very different approach. He has a miserable time at school; teased and ostracized by his fellow students, he fantasizes revenge. His opportunity comes when he returns to his old school as their young new teacher. In a series of audacious pranks he gets even with the children he dislikes.[15]

Children who are bullied generally divide fictional writers. Some stress the virtues of disengagement or deflection, while others champion standing up to a bully. In anti-revenge tales bullies realize they are doing wrong, or they are humoured, befriended, chased away by other children or thwarted by adults.[16] In pro-retaliation accounts the victim conquers their fear and cuts the bully down to size, or is portrayed as a hero for trying. Benjie in Betsy Byars's *The Eighteenth Emergency* is a nicely nuanced example.[17] In a finely textured tale, Benjie, aka 'Mouse', has the quirky habit of writing cryptic instructions on walls and objects, such as 'To open building tear along this line' beside a long crack in a plaster wall. At school one day he pauses by a large wall-chart depicting images of prehistoric man and absent-mindedly scribbles 'Marv Hammerman' on the chart, with an arrow pointing to the picture of Neanderthal man. But 'Neanderthal' Marv Hammerman, the school tough and bully, happens to be right behind him. Horrified, Benjie goes into rapid flight.

Hammerman puts word out that he wants revenge, and for days Benjie is tormented by the prospect of being beaten up. It gradually dawns on him that he has dishonoured Marv Hammerman: he did not mean to, but he really has, and it was now Hammerman's right to say when his honour was restored. So instead of hiding from him, Benjie, terrified, seeks him out for the inevitable thrashing. He is hopelessly outclassed as Hammerman pummels him, but then Hammerman suddenly stops and dismisses Benjie – honour retrieved. Benjie feels a huge weight lifted from his small, bruised shoulders. This tale does not glorify revenge, nor does it condemn it; there is a kind of moral balancing between Benjie's unthinking insult and Hammerman's retaliation. It would have been better, perhaps, if matters could have been resolved without resorting to violence, but in the febrile climate of the schoolyard justice is seen to be done and the dispute can now end.

The master-weaver of revenge tales Roald Dahl sides firmly with children who are ill-treated by adults. Authorities are not to be trusted, a recurring theme in his magically redemptive, wacky stories. In *Matilda*, the eponymous heroine responds to her verbally abusive, neglectful parents by squeezing superglue in her father's hat, putting bleach in his hair tonic and shoving the family parrot up the chimney. She also discovers her remarkable psychokinetic powers, propelling objects towards her much hated teacher. James, in *James and the Giant Peach*, also visits hell on abusive adults. Orphaned, he is sent to live with his cruel aunts where he is beaten and bullied. One day an old man gives him a gift of crocodile tongues, and James accidentally drops them on a peach tree, transforming it into a giant sprout inhabited by friendly insects. James escapes his aunts to live with his new friends, who then help him to squash the aunts with a giant peach – and float away.

Imaginative children's literature can explore revenge's uneven moral terrain in an engaging and colourful way. Why should we want to hurt one another? Is standing up for what you believe always a good thing? When can revenge make things better, and when much worse?

'NEVER WRONG a writer, they get their revenge in print', goes the adage. This chapter would be incomplete without mention of writers who use their literary skills to settle their personal scores. A. N. Wilson, while writing a biography of the late poet John Betjeman, was thrilled to receive a copy of a love letter that Betjeman had sent to an Honor Tracy. It revealed a previously unknown love tryst, and Wilson happily included it in his published biography. But then a journalist spotted an oddity: the first letter of each sentence of the epistle was a code that spelled out 'A. N. Wilson is a shit'. The self-confessed culprit was Bevis Hillier. Hillier was incensed at Wilson's insulting review of his own published biography of John Betjeman. Wilson described Hillier's book as a 'hopeless mishmash . . . Some reviewers would say it was badly written, but the trouble is, it isn't really written at all. It is hurled together.' Hillier's revenge was, accordingly, very sweet.'[18]

In the thin-skinned world of writers, the fictive and the personal can meld. Lightly disguised fictional characters can be used

to wound or embarrass actual adversaries. Crime fict
Peter James created a villainous character called Amis
for his novel *Not Yet Dead* (2012). Smallbone, end
arrogance and a tiny penis, represented James's nemesis, Martin
Amis. James had studied with Amis but, as James relates, Amis
perfunctorily dismissed him at a book award ceremony, suggest-
ing pompously that James's interest in him was solely because
of Amis's own fame.[19] Another example is *Broken Trust* (2014),
Shannon Baker's second novel, in which most of the characters
suffer humiliation or an untimely death. Baker confessed that
they were modelled on ex-colleagues: she could not resist her
'writerly urge for revenge on distasteful ex-co-workers'.[20]

A personal romantic disaster can truly sharpen a writer's
literary claws. Poet Louise Colet had a tumultuous adulterous
relationship with Gustave Flaubert, which ended rancorously.
Flaubert then based his sexually explicit *Madame Bovary* on their
romantic affair, importing intimate details, including their first
erotic encounter in a carriage. All this was too much for Colet, who
retaliated in her successful novel *Lui, roman contemporain* (1859).
In it a character resembling Flaubert is shown as a horny woman-
izer, exploiter and buffoon. Norman Mailer also had revenge in
mind when he penned his misogynistic *An American Dream*
(1965). His tempestuous marriage to his third wife, Jean Campbell,
failed after his infidelity. Their rows, quipped Campbell, could
'empty a room quicker than anyone in New York'. Her double in
An American Dream had a violent quarrel with her estranged
husband, who strangled her in his rage and then threw her body
off the tenth-floor balcony to make it look like an accident.
Campbell described the work as 'the hate book of all time'.[21]

Mailer's venom is palpable, but is trounced by Ernest Hemingway. In 1940 Hemingway divorced his second wife so that

1e could marry Martha Gellhorn, an attractive, intelligent journalist and accomplished fiction writer. Five years later, plagued by Hemingway's jealousies and bullying, Gellhorn walked out on him: 'Why should I be a footnote to somebody else's life?'[22] Hemingway found it hard to accept that he was married to a talented career woman who did not want to languish at home to serve his needs. He could not forgive her for abandoning him, so he struck back contemptuously in writings. In one work, a poem, there was no attempt at disguise: 'To Martha Gellhorn's Vagina'. The poem likened said organ to the crumpled neck of an old hot water bottle. And in a post-war story, 'It Was Very Cold in England', a Hemingway-like character compares the sexual performance of a Gellhorn-like character to a washed-up mine that had failed to detonate.[23] His rancour continued even after he had remarried. In *Across the River and into the Trees* Gellhorn's ghost is visible in the main character's assessment of his wife: 'She had more ambition than Napoleon and about the talent of the average High School Valedictorian . . . [d]eader than Phoebus the Phoenician. But she doesn't know it yet.'[24]

The literary merits of these personal vendettas are arguable. On the one hand they can be seen as enriching the author's narrative and can do no great harm when the characters, or literary devices, are well disguised. On the other hand, they can appear a prostitution of the writer's art, a pernicious self-indulgence that ensures that retribution on specific victims will remain on public record for a very long time.

FOUR

EYES, TEETH AND JUSTICE

Jean-Vincent Scheil had the good fortune to be there in 1901 when the sensational discovery was made. He was attached to an archaeological mission excavating the ruins at Susa, Iran. They unearthed a stone pillar, or stele, eight feet high and weighing four tons, covered in cuneiform inscriptions. Scheil, a friar by vocation, was also a qualified Egyptologist and Assyriologist and in less than a year he had translated the text. It revealed 282 laws of the Babylonian King Hammurabi (*r. c.* 1792–1750 BC), addressing matters of civic life from criminal behaviour to property rights, divorce and slavery. It was Hammurabi's attempt to control his sprawling empire and the chaos of vigilante justice. The stele was not the earliest legal codification, but it was by far the most elaborate, and now resides in the Louvre as one of its prized possessions.[1] It set in stone, literally, the law of talion – 'an eye for an eye' – for certain crimes and was clearly intended for public display, a powerful symbol of authority. The state had appropriated revenge: justice was the state's prerogative, not the individual's.

Hammurabi's laws were, ostensibly, a fair deal for all, but, in practice, existing social divisions meant that not everyone was treated equally. An upper-class Babylonian who took the eye of an equal would have to sacrifice his own eye, but if he blinded a commoner it cost him just sixty shekels. If a doctor killed a wealthy patient he would lose his hands, but if the victim was a slave he would only have to pay a fine. Punishment for thieving was similarly status-calibrated. Stealing a cow, sheep, ass, pig or goat from the gentry meant a fine of thirty times the beast's value, but it was no more than tenfold if the owner was an ordinary commoner. Should the thief not have the wherewithal to meet a fine, which was highly likely in crimes of poverty, then the unfortunate soul could be put to death.[2]

By the Middle Ages brutal justice was well institutionalized, although, surrounded by miserable wars, plagues and famines, the average citizen would have been no stranger to physical suffering. 'Ordeals' – trials by fire, water or combat – were common, fusing man's cruelty to 'God's will'. In a fire ordeal a suspect had to walk a prescribed distance grasping a red-hot iron. The hand was then bound for three days, after which a priest determined whether, by the grace of God, it had healed sufficiently to prove innocence; a still-festering wound could mean execution or exile.[3] A variation required walking barefoot across red-hot ploughshares, the fate of Emma of Normandy, wife of Edward the Confessor, accused of an amorous affair with the Bishop of Winchester. According to legend, the night before her ordeal she witnessed a vision of St Swithin, who informed her that she would walk free. It proved a reliable prophecy because she strode the glowing ploughshares without murmur, her feet uninjured. Her reward was humble forgiveness from Edward, plus reinstatement of her title and property.[4]

Water ordeals varied. In one version, the suspect had to plunge their hand into a cauldron of boiling water and, like the fire ordeal, be judged according to their wounds after several days. In another the accused, legs and arms bound, was lowered into a cold pool, pond or river. If they sank, God had received them and they were innocent. If they floated it was God's rejection and they would be punished: by the removal of their eyes, limbs or sexual organs. As these ordeals were tests of God's will, the Church had more than a passing interest in their administration and, as a contemporary manual informs us, the ritual was often meticulous:

If anyone has been accused of theft and he denies having done it, on Tuesday at vespers let him be led to the church for the purpose of purging himself, clothed in woollen garments and walking barefoot; and there, that is in the church, let him remain until the sabbath day . . .

On the sabbath . . . let the man be stripped not only of his woollen garments, but also of his undergarments, and let him be girded about the loins with new linen cloth, lest his genitals be seen, and let him be covered until the hour or time with a cloak or cape because of the cold; and so let him be led to the pool of water with procession and litany . . .

Let the pool of water be twelve feet in depth and about twenty in width, and let it be filled to the top with water. Over a third part of the pit let there be put strong boards with a strong hurdle, to hold up the priest blessing the water and the judges standing by and the man about to enter the water, with two or three men lowering him in . . .

[L]et the accuser and the defendant swear oaths, such as those about to engage in judicial combat swear; and let the hands of the accused be tied together under his bent knees . . . Then let a rope strong enough to hold him be bound around his loins; and let there be made a knot in the rope at the length of his longer hair; and thus let him be lowered into the water gently, lest the water be disturbed.

If he sinks to the knot, let him be drawn out as saved; if not, however, let him be adjudged as guilty by those watching.[5]

Ordeal by combat was an offshoot of Anglo-Norman law where guilt or innocence was determined by a test of arms. A surviving loser would have to face state retribution, perhaps death by burning or hanging for a criminal offence, or loss of limbs or property for a civil felony. In England feuding parties could appoint 'champions' to fight on their behalf, a practice that spawned a murky industry of freelancers who sold their fighting services to the highest bidder. They were useful, but not exactly prestigious, regarded on a par with prostitutes, bastards and actors.[6] The clergy, banned from combat, were known to avail themselves of their services to resolve personal disputes. In 1258 the Abbot of Glastonbury hired one Henry of Fernbureg for thirty marks to help him settle a long quarrel with the bishop and chapter of Bath and Wells: ten marks at the time of waging the duel, five on his being shaven, the rest 'to be placed in the hands of some good man who was to pay it over to Henry if he struck so much as one stroke in the duel'.[7] And in 1289 Bishop Swinefeld of Hereford kept a champion on call for a retainer of 6s. 8d. a year.[8] English law also gave the Crown the right to appoint a convicted criminal as a champion or 'approver', who was willing to fight a fellow felon. If he triumphed he could be granted a reduced sentence or even a pardon.

Combat protocol prescribed how combatants should be armed, what they should wear, the place of the contest, the dimensions of the duelling ground and the time allowed for the contest. Ordeals could be gruelling, ending with the last man standing or a clear sign of surrender.[9] On 11 April 1127 two high-status combatants confronted each other in the grounds of a Flanders manor. They were well armed and mounted. Their dispute concerned the murder of Charles the Good, Count of Flanders, who was hacked to death by a group of knights as he knelt at prayer in church. Herman the Iron accused Guy of Steenvoorde of being a conspirator and challenged him to combat. An eyewitness provides a vivid account of what happened:

> Everyone present went out to the manor where the combat between Herman the Iron and Guy had been called and where both sides fought bitterly. Guy had unhorsed his adversary and kept him down with his lance just as he liked whenever Herman tried to get up. Then his adversary, coming closer, disembowelled Guy's horse, running him through with his sword. Guy, having slipped from his horse, rushed at his adversary with his sword drawn.
>
> Now there was a continuous and bitter struggle, with alternating thrusts of swords, until both, exhausted by the weight and burden of arms, threw away their shields and hastened to gain victory in the fight by resorting to wrestling. Herman the Iron fell prostrate on the ground, and Guy was lying on top of him, smashing the knight's face and eyes with his iron gauntlets. But Herman, prostrate, little by little regained his strength by the coolness of the earth ... and by cleverly lying quiet made Guy believe he was certain of victory. Meanwhile, gently moving his hand down to the lower edge of the cuirass [breastplate]

where Guy was not protected, Herman seized him by the testicles, and summoning all his strength for the brief space of one moment he hurled Guy from him; by this tearing motion all of the lower parts of the body were broken so that Guy, now prostrate, gave up, crying out that he was conquered and dying.[10]

Guy's agony ended on the gallows, sharing a gibbet with the corpse of another of the conspirators.

Women were conspicuous by their absence from combat ordeals, but there were exceptions. In Germany, for instance, a rancorous or irreconcilable marriage could be settled by physical battle between the feuding couple. Germanic law was precise in evening out the odds. In one arrangement the man was put into a pit up to his waist, a hand tied behind his back, and then armed with three wooden clubs. His wife could run freely around the pit with her weapons: three small rocks of predetermined weight, each tied in a small sack. If the man touched the edge of the pit he would have to sacrifice one of his cudgels while his wife backed off. Should she fail to, she forfeited one of her rocks. Early drawings show wild manoeuvrings, including choking, testicle-grabbing and clubbing. The man triumphed if he managed to haul the woman into the pit; the woman won if she dragged him out. Alternatively, sheer mutilation of the other party could bring the combat to an end. A surviving loser would then face sentencing by the state: beheading for a man, loss of the right hand for a woman.[11]

Justice in the Middle Ages mirrored the feudal system. The monarch held absolute power, presiding over his barons, earls and dukes. The peasantry – villeins, serfs and slaves – had little or no voice and were subject to the gentry's interests or whims. The

Church weighed in with its own tax demands on peasants, many of whom were required to work on church lands for free. Ballads of the time roundly reviled them as 'insolent', 'tricky', 'unshaved', 'unwashed', 'foul smelling' and 'ugly'.[12] They were compelled to swear allegiance to their lord, and any violations could bring harsh reprisals, so few dared resist. When they finally did, however, in the 1381 Peasants' Revolt, it so unnerved the boy king, Richard II, that he commissioned a force of some 4,000 troops to suppress it. He is reported to have turned on a delegation of rebels with the words, 'Rustics you were and rustics you are still. You will remain in bondage, not as before, but incomparably harsher. For as long as we live we will strive to suppress you and your misery will be an example for posterity.'[13] An unambiguous message of power and subjugation.

Knights, too, were obliged to pledge fealty to their lord – to protect his property, collect taxes from the serfs on the estate and enlist them in military service when required. Contrary to their romanticized image, they were a motley bunch, fighting each other for territory, launching revenge attacks and contemptuous of any peasants who got in their way.[14] Their masters, the barons, earls and dukes, were unquestionably powerful, but were themselves beholden to the monarch. Displeasing the king could bring dire consequences, such as confiscation of their lands, titles or worse. William de Braose, 4th Lord of Bramber, is a case in point. He was a ruthless and ambitious man, dubbed the Ogre of Abergavenny for his merciless dealings with his enemies. To King John he could do no wrong, until, that is, a disagreement about monies he supposedly owed to the Crown. De Braose went on the run, and in revenge the King seized his estates and took his wife and eldest son hostage. He imprisoned them in the dungeon of Corfe Castle, Dorset, where, according to chroniclers of the time, they died of starvation, the son's corpse bearing the bite marks of his desperate mother.[15]

Corporal punishment defined the era. A wife was considered the property of her husband, so she could be beaten 'for her own correction; for she is of his household'.[16] Thieves and pickpockets lost their hands; poisoners were boiled alive; tortured bodies, decapitated heads and corpses were put on public display – a deterrent that substituted for weak or non-existent policing. A rapist could be flogged, castrated, blinded or executed, although a rape victim made pregnant did not find it easy to get justice. Apart from the misogyny of all male juries, there was a folk belief that a woman could conceive only if she secreted a special seed, and that was only possible if she experienced sexual satisfaction. A woman pregnant from an alleged rape must, therefore, have enjoyed the encounter, so she could not have been raped, an early rendition of 'she brought it on herself'.[17]

By the middle of the sixteenth century political turbulence and recession characterized much of Europe. England was plagued by high inflation, unemployment and failed harvests, ideal conditions for creating scapegoats. The country lived 'in terror of the tramp', as historian R. H. Tawney put it. The Vagrancy Act of 1547 made it illegal for an able-bodied man to be out of work for more than three days, on pain of branding with a 'V'. Vagabonds were 'arrested, whipped until bloody, and returned by the most direct route to their place of origin'.[18] Some were enslaved or bonded into labour. A central plank of justice was public shaming. The beggar, the drunk, the short-changer, the insulter of royalty, the blasphemer, the perjurer, the fraudster or the homosexual would be committed to the pillories, stocks or ladders for hours or days. Eggs, dung, mud or offal were favoured missiles, stones reserved for the especially loathed. In this way local communities became de facto state agents in the administration of justice.

The full wrath of the state was unleashed on traitors. The punishment for high treason in England, which lasted well into the eighteenth century, was public beheading or being hanged, drawn and quartered. But why these particular assaults on the traitor's body? After their failed plot to assassinate King James in 1605, Guy Fawkes and his fellow conspirators were hanged, drawn and quartered. The Attorney General, Sir Edward Coke, described in detail what such punishment meant:

after a traitor hath had his just trial and is convicted and attainted, he shall have his judgment, to be [horse] drawn to the place of execution from his prison, as being not worthy any more to tread upon the face of the earth whereof he was made: also for that he hath been retrograde to nature, therefore is he drawn backward at a horse-tail. And whereas God hath made the head of man the highest and most supreme part, as being his chief grace and ornament, he must be drawn with his head declining downward, and lying so near the ground as may be, being thought unfit to take benefit of the common air; for which cause he shall be strangled, being hanged up by the neck between heaven and earth, as deemed unworthy of both or either; as likewise, that the eyes of men may behold, and their hearts condemn him. His bowels and inward parts taken out and burnt, who inwardly had conceived and harboured in his heart such horrible treason. After to have his head cut off, which had imagined the mischief. And lastly, his body to be quartered, and the quarters set up in some high and eminent place, to the view and detestation of men, and to become a prey for the fowls of the air.[19]

It is doubtful whether onlookers would have appreciated all this symbolism, but the general message about the penalty for treason would surely have struck home.

SINCE THE eighteenth century criminal justice reformers have worked to shift the balance away from punitive retribution towards education, rehabilitation and restorative justice. Capital punishment rarely makes us any safer and few would-be killers are deterred by it.[20] The talion, nevertheless, lives on in many parts of the globe. In the USA 31 states retained the death penalty in 2015, dividing a Christian nation into two. God, quipped one wit, appears as 'a large, male, sheriff with a gun . . . ready to retaliate against anybody he doesn't like'.[21] In that year more than fifty countries prescribed the death penalty for a brutal murder, delivered by lethal injection, hanging, beheading, firing squad or stoning.[22] Some nations included large-scale corruption, adultery, sexual offences and drug dealing. In a startling move in 2016, the president of the Philippines declared his approval for the extrajudicial killing of drug users, leading to thousands of summary executions on the street. State justice and revenge are close bedfellows and, at times, hard to tell apart. Revenge simmers away beneath the civilized veneer of justice, and it wants out.

FIVE

TRIBES AND BLOODY HONOUR

When a tribe is attacked, its land taken, kin violated or honour impugned, revenge is natural justice. It inflicts costs on the perpetrators and acts as a warning to them and others to keep off. Some threats are more inflammatory than others, so tribal revenge contains its own checks and balances. Killing is normally reserved for high-impact transgressions, such as murder, clashes over land ownership or precious animals.[1] In the late 1990s a feud between two mountain tribes in remote Western New Guinea began when a tribal chief was killed in battle, but could not end until the head of the other tribe had been slain – a quid pro quo. Sexual infidelities, the seduction of another man's wife, reneging on a promised girl for marriage or the forced capture of women can trigger major disputes – because they can jeopardize the cohesion, kin structure or reproductive capacity of a tribe.[2]

Revenge can act as a brake on conflict, but invariably some feuds get out of hand. In 2013 the Ukupa Kuwar and the Kulga tribes in Papua New Guinea had been at each other's throats for decades, the cause but dim memory; elders vaguely recalled a dispute over women. The conflict was so culturally embedded that there was a regular 'fight day' every few months at an agreed spot. Resembling a line-up of medieval armies, hundreds of warriors faced each other in mortal combat for several hours, and then retired. 'We can't create peace and stop the fight,' declared one fighter, 'because our enemy does not want to stop, and neither do we' – a self-reinforcing logic we now regularly hear in communities locked into intractable conflicts.[3]

Modern weapons are a game changer in tribal disputes, 'from spears to M-16s', as anthropologist Polly Wiessner describes it.[4] Traditional cudgels, machetes and bows and arrows can be lethal, but feeble in comparison to modern weapons, which can spell a tribe's annihilation.[5] This was almost the case for the Enga people, a clan-divided community in the Southern Highlands of New Guinea. Warring and revenge are deeply rooted in their history, although they have had some peaceful times. In the nineteenth century they agreed that disputes could be settled by compensation rather than violence: the forfeit of pigs, a prized Enga staple. But that changed when Papua New Guinea gained independence from Australia in the late twentieth century. To the consternation of many Engas, hot-headed tribal youths acquired high-powered rifles traded on the black market. Revenge attacks were now indiscriminate and clan leaders lost control in the runaway violence. By 2005 a war-weary and impoverished Enga community decided they would shun the vigilante warriors and return to village courts, reinstating traditional forms of compensation. The pigs, once again, had their day.[6]

Clan revenge proliferates when state law is absent or weak, particularly in remoter regions and island communities. It has been thus in Corsica, Sicily, Sardinia, the deserts of North Africa, the Balkans, feudal Japan, medieval Iceland and the ancient Scottish Highlands. Corsica's deadly feuds peaked between 1682 and 1714 with more than 28,000 recorded deaths out of a population of only 120,000: family insults and killings had to be repaid in blood.[7] Risking one's life may seem a steep price to pay to defend one's personal reputation or family name, but the costs of doing nothing were regarded as much greater. Corsican mothers would remind their sons of their sacred duty to avenge a family death, pinning bloodstained pieces of the slain person's shirt to their sons' clothing and chanting songs of revenge over the dead body.[8] A rugged landscape of austere granite houses lent itself to a fortress mentality where warring families could plot their revenge. Officially, Corsica's last vendetta occurred in 1954 at a village near Ajaccio, over a seemingly trivial incident: a donkey strayed into a neighbour's garden. In the ensuing conflict the garden owner was killed and the murderer served a period in jail, to later die of natural causes. But that did not quench the thirst for revenge. At the man's funeral, passions exploded in a shoot-out between the warring families, killing one person and wounding six others.[9] Nowadays Corsican vendettas have transmuted into mafia-style banditry and killings linked to the struggle for independence from Corsica's colonial ruler, France. Significantly, these are reported in the local press as *règlement de comptes*, 'settling scores'.

Tribal revenge is frequently defined by unwritten codes. In Afghanistan, for instance, Pashtuns are the largest ethnic group in a nation comprising three competing judicial systems: custom, religion and the state. Pashtunwali is a pre-Islamic customary code passed down through generations, exerting a strong moral influence over Pashtun communities.[10] It covers courage, hospitality, loyalty and honour, and states that some insults demand the shedding of blood, no matter how long it takes. Indeed, one feud lasted for thirty years in an Afghan settlement in Nangarhar province, ending only after the intervention of the provincial governor in 2008; by then 318 people had lost their lives and most families were blighted. 'It started over Sambola's widow,' explained the leader of one of the sides. 'Ashmir Khan was supposed to marry her. But Haji Nasruddin Khan married her instead. Ashmir shot Nasruddin, and that is how it began.' The feud spread across the settlement and into nearby settlements, dividing people along clan lines. Homes turned into fortifications: 'In order to leave the village you had to wait until midnight or later to creep away in the dark', said one clan member, 'and sometimes they would have ambushes for you'. He lost six members of his family. Women were protected under the Pashtunwali code and they, in a reverse of the usual gender order, ended up running the village.[11]

In Albania the Kanun has functioned similarly to Pashtunwali. Dating back to the fifteenth century, it was initially an oral set of codes, but in the nineteenth century it was transcribed to comprise twelve books on rules of behaviour, including honour and revenge. An honour violation could be a personal insult, a property dispute, disrespecting a woman, accusing a person of lying, an accidental killing or a murder. It was customary to formally announce an honour feud in the village, and then hand responsibility for its execution to the victim's closest male relative.

Under the communist regime of Enver Hoxha, the Albanian state banned the Kanun, but after Hoxha's fall it resurfaced in remoter parts of the country. In 2012, 118 honour killings were recorded, and 1,600 families were believed to be in hiding.[12] Leonard Qukaj was among them. It all started in 2010 with a dispute over a watermill in the mountains where his family once lived. The water flowed through a neighbouring property, that of the Prroj family, and they wanted payment for the facility. Leonard's uncle took this as an insult and shot and killed a Prroj family member in revenge. The Prrojs took counter-revenge two years later, killing two of the Qukajs. The feud continued, taking with it Leonard's seventeen-year-old cousin as she tended her grandfather's field. Eventually, in fear for his life, Leonard was forced into hiding, shut away with little to do. In April 2014 Leonard's uncle 'did his duty'; sporting a Kalashnikov, he sprayed the Prroj clan leader with bullets. 'Reconciliation,' says Leonard with grim resignation, 'will never happen.'[13]

'YOUR HONOR is your pride, your glory and praise. You can be without water or food. You can live without water or food but you cannot live on without honor.' These are the words of a man serving a prison sentence for an honour killing.[14] For those who do not share its cultural immersion, honour killing is hard to grasp. The practice is more cultural than religious, although there are distinct clusters among some Muslim and migrant Muslim communities. Most victims are women living in gender-unequal communities and families where there is strong patriarchal control. There are, according to the United Nations Population Fund, some 5,000 victims a year. Women cannot increase the honour of their group or family, but they can reduce it by their 'irrational' or 'immoral' behaviour, a disgrace that has to be eradicated. Navi Pillay, ex-High Commissioner for Human Rights, does not mince her words: 'In the name of preserving family "honour", women and girls are shot, stoned, burned, buried alive, strangled, smothered and knifed to death with horrifying regularity.'[15] Unlike other femicide, honour killing is typically a family project involving brothers, uncles, fathers and, occasionally, female relatives. The victim will be depersonalized and demonized, clearing the pathway to her ejection or destruction. Some are pressed into taking their own lives and provided with the means, such as poison, a noose or a gun.[16]

Shame plays a pivotal role in honour vengeance. Shame exists in all societies but, as anthropologist Ruth Benedict pointed out in the 1940s, it is deeply entrenched in some cultures. Asian shame, for instance, hinges upon the fear of rejection and the loss of support from family and community. The perception of others, what they think of you, is vital. Dishonour brings shame to the whole extended family and a daughter who shames the family by, say, premarital sex or refusing an arranged marriage, carries the burden of her own and her family's ignominy. Her expulsion or death is a way of wiping out the shame, a cleansing.

Traditional Bedouin life encapsulates these principles. Bedouins are semi-nomadic, patriarchal Arabs who have long roamed the deserts of the Middle East and North Africa. Chastity and sexual purity are drummed into Bedouin girls at an early age, preparing them for their future roles as wives. For a Bedouin man schooled in Islam, his wife and daughter are more than his responsibility; they are his honour and possessions. Just as newlyweds in the West set up home, Bedouins will 'set up a tent' to symbolize their marriage union, a sanctuary in a hostile environment. Its inhabitants are to be protected by its owner. Any violation of a daughter's or wife's honour is akin to the destruction of the tent and a source of profound shame for the family head. It undermines his control and standing in the community. Violent revenge and honour killing are accepted correctives: Bedouin custom permits the killing of a married woman who has illicit sexual relations, and if she is caught in flagrante, her husband has the right to slay both parties.[17]

Many Bedouins have forsaken their nomadic ways for an urban lifestyle, but tribal honour remains. Israel, for example, is home to some quarter of a million Bedouins in rural villages. A generation of young Bedouin women live part of their life in a liberal, Westernized environment, and part in a culture of powerful kinship ties and rigid honour protocols. Clashes are inevitable and periodically honour killings are reported in the Israeli press (although there is reluctance by the Israeli authorities to use the 'honour' designation in their crime statistics).[18] In 2014, for example, an Arab woman's husband, ex-husband and brother were convicted of her honour killing; she was the tenth woman in the family to die that way. The police described the victim as an independent and dominant woman, but 'her husband and brother didn't like that'.[19] In another instance, a fifteen-year-old girl was stabbed to death by her brother in a suspected honour killing in the Bedouin town of Tel Sheva. She had been dating a boy against the wishes of her family and had refused to sever ties with him.[20] And, in a third example, a Bedouin father was the prime suspect in the murder of his sixteen-year-old daughter over an 'undesirable romantic involvement'. Her body was found in a well in the Kuseife community in the Negev. Her father refused to cooperate in the investigation. In his summing up, the judge noted that 'the family is maintaining a conspiracy of silence. This is the gravest offence in the rulebook. When it's an "honor killing" it makes it even worse.'[21]

Honour reprisals in Western Europe and North America began to surface in the 1990s when the children of first-generation immigrants began to assimilate, but their parents and grand-parents continued to embrace their traditional ways. In the UK more than 11,000 honour crimes were recorded by police forces between 2010 and 2014, daughters the main victims. A recurring theme has been the clash between the dominant culture's free-doms and the predetermined life choices of imported customs.[22]

Naila Afsar fled the family home in Bradford in the UK in 2009 to escape the prospect of a forced marriage with her cousin, and she secretly married the man of her choice. Her mother described her as 'worse than a prostitute'. The family drugged and abducted her, but she survived and her kidnappers – mother, brother and brother-in-law – were all jailed.[23] Samia Shahid, also from Bradford, married the man she wanted, but only after divorcing her cousin, the man she was forced to marry. Her family in Bradford and Pakistan were insulted and shamed. In 2016 they lured her over to Pakistan, where they demanded that she change her mind. She refused. On the day before she was to return to the UK she was strangled by her first husband, who was aided by her father. Her second husband, distraught at hearing of her 'sudden heart attack', flew immediately to Pakistan and filed a criminal complaint against the family. The perpetrators were charged with her murder.[24]

In Texas, teenage sisters Amina and Sarah Said were shot dead by their Egyptian-born father on New Year's Day 2008, their bodies left in a cab at a hotel parking lot. They had tried to escape his suffocating control and his attempts to marry them off to men of his choice in Egypt, one of whom was nearly fifty. The case inspired a feature documentary, *The Price of Honor*.[25] In Georgia that same year the body of 25-year-old Sandeela Kanwal was found on the floor of her bedroom. Her Pakistani father confessed that he had strangled her because she wanted to leave an arranged marriage, which he said brought shame to the family and betrayed both her religion and her husband.[26]

In 2014 a European Convention for combating violence against women came into force, a resolution that included honour killing. There was 'no honour in killing'. In his introduction to the Convention, Secretary General Thorbjørn Jagland stated that, 'We cannot accept cultural excuses for any form of violence based on so-called honour.'[27] By early 2017 thirteen member states had ratified the Convention, and agreed to provide helplines, counselling and shelters. As generations change and assimilate, the pull of traditional honour codes is likely to weaken, but effective policies on cultural integration and gender equality remain crucial.

ONCE UPON a time honour had a rather different face: chivalric. It extolled qualities such as gallantry towards women, bravery and courtesy, and was something of an obsession among the European upper classes between the sixteenth and eighteenth centuries. Pure honour separated an upstanding gentleman from the hoi polloi, and any challenge to honour had to be defended at all costs. The duel was the favoured method, civilizing revenge in a ritualized contest of class equals.

The very act of 'calling out' an offender, and 'demanding satisfaction', was the pinnacle of male courage, and a first step towards recovering honour. Duels with swords or pistols could be lethal, but killing an opponent was not specifically the intention. The bible of duelling etiquette, *The Code Duello*, laid out the principles.[28] A genuine apology delivered before or during a duel could settle the difference: 'Seconds are bound to attempt reconciliation before the meeting takes place or after sufficient firing or hits, as specified.' A wound could halt proceedings: 'Any wound sufficient to agitate the nerves and necessarily make the hand shake, must end the business for that day.' And a duel could end when one party was 'well blooded, disabled, or disarmed . . . or after receiving a wound, and blood being drawn, the aggressor begs pardon'.

By the nineteenth century the social exclusiveness of the duel was weakening. When two Berlin waiters fought a duel in 1870 they were imprisoned for their presumptuousness, the Prussian Minister of Justice remarking that they 'belong to a class of society in which it is not customary to settle one's affairs by duel'.[29] But, just as serious, the very essence of honour was shifting; it was becoming feral – any difference, slight or bar-room quarrel could be an excuse for a duel. An Irish eccentric, George Fitzgerald, epitomized the new order. He was dubbed 'Fighting Fitzgerald' for his savage temper and habit of rushing to duel. His not infrequent brushes with the law resulted in a period in prison, but that did not dull his appetite for duelling. On his release he contrived revenge against the very barrister who helped convict him, by shooting dead his pet wolfhound. The dismayed barrister, a committed animal protector and skilled shooter, challenged him to a duel. Both were injured in the contest.[30]

In the late nineteenth century chivalric honour fell from favour; serious personal feuds transferred to the courts, the spilling of words rather than blood. Honour, however, had not disappeared but was being reshaped by new players: urban tribes in the shape of street gangs. Street gangs, now commonplace, operate in the shadowy crevices of cityscapes. They frequently structure themselves along feudal lines – baronies, booty, victimization and punishments – and are intent on protecting their territory and status: insult met with insult, attack with revenge. A gang member's standing is dependent on their willingness to use force to defend their own and the gang's honour.

In the 1920s sociologist Frederic Thrasher described how Chicago gang feuds took on a life of their own, a subsociety where 'hatred, and thirst for revenge are continually stimulated by repeated insults and aggression. A killing by one side calls for a killing by the other.'[31] Nearly a century later Thrasher's portrayal remains apposite. Street gangs have proliferated, competing for the most profitable territory and gains: drugs, theft, muggings, weapons.[32] The typical recruit is a male youth from a broken or violent family, unsure about his identity or future.

The gang fills the vacuum, providing prestige, racial or ethnic identity, companionship, respect and money. The gang is empowering: power to impress, power to buy things and power to exact revenge. None of this comes of right; a new member is usually exposed to harsh initiation ('sexed in' for girls), then required to prove themselves by doing whatever a senior member of the gang wants. Loyalty and 'respect' bond gang members, and gangland etiquette sensitizes them to the slightest sign that they are not getting the respect they believe they deserve, which demands retaliation.[33] A Californian gang member described the reasoning:

> The only thing we can do is build our own little nation. We know we have complete control in our community. It's like we're making our stand and we're able to express ourselves in this way. We're all brothers and nobody fucks with us . . . We take pride in our little nation and if any intruders enter, we get panicked because we feel our community is being threatened. The only way is with violence.[34]

A sobering conclusion, from many years of research, is that the forces that create and unite gang members are nearly always stronger than those that try to break them apart. The challenge is to find ways of reducing the initial attraction of gangs. Scare tactics tend not to work, such as showing children at risk what is in store for them in correctional institutions if they join a criminal gang.[35] Programmes that reach out to communities, working intensively and therapeutically with children and families in schools and homes, have been more promising.[36] But none of these can fix the underlying socio-economic factors that create an underclass of disaffected young people surrounded by poor housing, inadequate educational services and grim employment prospects. Here, changes in social policy are essential if gang violence and vengeance are to lose some of their appeal.

SIX

A VERY PERSONAL GRUDGE

In 2013 Vester Lee Flanagan, upset and uttering threats, was escorted from the small Virginian TV station where he worked. He had been sacked following several reprimands about his unprofessional conduct. Two years later he reappeared, carrying a gun. He calmly approached two of his ex-colleagues conducting a live interview and shot them dead, wounding the interviewee. He then fled the scene and killed himself, but not before posting a video of his attack on Twitter together with a long account of his grievances. The whole episode could not have been more public, beamed live on TV and circulated on social media.

Grudges, psychologists tell us, are persistent feelings of ill will or resentment resulting from a past insult or injury. Vester Lee Flanagan truly fitted this description. He had lost his court case for wrongful dismissal and, in his suicide confessions, insisted that he been racially slurred and victimized by his former colleagues. He also recounted decades-old grievances about once being attacked and bullied for being black and gay. His final written words encapsulated his frenzied state of mind: 'a human powder keg . . . just waiting to go BOOM!!! at any moment'.

SOME EVENTS cut deeply into our pride and self-esteem: an unfair dismissal, being cheated or swindled, a humiliation. We cannot 'just let it go'. A lover's betrayal can feel like a stab to the heart, a breach of trust that is impossible to shake off or forgive. Revenge can seem the only true justice: the betrayer must suffer as you have by a retaliatory affair ('if he can do it so can I'), sexual withdrawal, physical attack or blackmail. Children can be caught in the crossfire, turned against their father or mother, or subject to kidnapping. Some victims choose to publicly humiliate their antagonist, like the American housewife who erected a large banner on her front lawn with the words: 'CHEATING HUSBAND. While his devoted wife was taking care of his sick Mother, Linnie was having affairs with two women at the same time.' And another sprayed her sentiments boldly across the bonnet of his car: 'HOPE THE PUSSY WAS WORTH IT! BASTARD.'[1] Infidelity arouses raw passions.

In these circumstances, women are generally less inclined to respond violently; but not always. In 1993 a Virginian housewife, Lorena Bobbitt, hit the headlines with her precisely targeted revenge. She grabbed a kitchen knife and sliced off her drunken husband's member. She fled with it in her car and tossed it into a field. It was later retrieved and, in a miracle of modern surgery, reattached to its original owner. Her action, she explained, was in response to years of sexual abuse by her husband who openly boasted of his infidelities – and a jury sympathized with her predicament. She later became a champion of abused women. Other penis severers have been treated less charitably. In 2013 Californian Catherine Kieu ensured that her cheating, sexually abusive husband would sexually perform no more. She sliced off his penis and ground it in her kitchen waste disposal unit. She was found guilty of torture, motivated by 'vengeance, vanity and jealousy', and given a life sentence.[2] And in China in 2013, Feng Lung stumbled across phone messages from her husband to his secret lover. Incandescent with rage, she grabbed a pair of scissors, stormed into the bedroom where he was sleeping, and snipped off his penis. He was rushed to hospital where the offending organ was sewn back on – but not for long. Feng Lung sneaked into his hospital room and repeated her efforts, this time throwing the penis out of the window. It was, it is believed, consumed by a stray dog or cat. She was arrested for grievous bodily harm and sentenced to a long jail term.[3]

Misogyny stacks the justice cards against abused women. In 2014 the Organisation for Economic Co-operation and Development listed more than sixty countries that had laws that were discriminatory towards women, or where family or religious customs conflicted with civil codes on gender equality.[4] An abused woman was compelled to keep silent or face a harsh backlash. In Turkey, for example, Islamic conservatism sits uneasily with state moves towards the greater inclusivity of women. Feminists are frequently vilified and life can be difficult for a woman who wants birth control or an abortion. 'It is open season if you see a woman who's not dressed modestly,' says gender relations specialist Professor Deniz Kandiyoti. Turkish journalist Cicek Tahaoglu elaborates:

> When a woman wears a miniskirt she deserves to get raped. When a woman doesn't do cooking and taking care of children . . . some men think she deserves to die. One case I will never forget. A man killed his wife with a cooking pan because there wasn't enough salt in the meal.[5]

Women who directly retaliate in such cultures are typically desperate. Nevin Yildirim is a case in point. She lived in a village in the southwestern Turkish province of Isparta and was secretly carrying an unwanted pregnancy, the result of a rape at gunpoint by a local worker. He had assaulted her in her home while her husband was away, and returned a number of times, usually drunk, to continue his abuse. He would, she said, beat her and threaten to kill her children if she complained. He boasted of his sexual exploits around the village, compounding her shame. She feared going to the police because she was convinced that they would not take her seriously. Then, on 20 August 2012 the man appeared once more with his gun, but this time she could take no more. She refused to let him in. He started to break in, so she grabbed a hunting rifle off the wall and shot him: 'He fell on the ground,' she said. 'He started swearing at me. I shot his sexual organ this time. He became quiet. I knew he was dead.' Then, in an act worthy of a Jacobean tragedy, she cut off his head. According to witnesses she carried the head to the village square, declaring to a stunned audience of men: 'Don't talk behind my back, don't play with my honour. Here's the head of the man who played with my honour.'[6]

When her case came to court she was unrepentant and said she would rather die than have the baby (abortion is rarely permitted in Turkey). Given the clear mitigating circumstances, the court's verdict was startling: because her 'romantic affair' was 'consensual' she was sentenced to life imprisonment. It provoked a sharp backlash from women's lawyers and feminist groups, accusing the legislature of yet further gender prejudice. Social media petitions sprang up in her defence and called for her release. They failed. 'This is a male-dominated country where codes of honour run deep,' writes Elif Shafak, a prominent observer of Turkish culture, 'and it is always women who pay the price – women, and at times their innocent children.'[7]

There are South Asian countries where male preference begins early on. Sons are welcome because they are expected to support their parents financially, look after the property and continue the family's patriarchal lineage and religious affiliation. In contrast, daughters are more of a financial burden, destined to be married off with expensive dowries. In some parts of India families avoid girls by infanticide or sex selection, and girls at the rump of a line of only daughters are subject to neglect.[8] Against this backdrop, Indian women in the rural hinterlands are typically fatalistic about their lot and the abuse they receive from men. In cities sexual harassment, euphemized as 'Eve-teasing', is commonplace and some women feel they need to protect themselves with concealed weapons, such as knives or safety pins.

Change for women has been slow in India. Rape cases can last for years, or never come to court, with the police inclined to blame the victim rather than arrest the perpetrator.[9] It has led to a number of women taking the law into their own hands. A dramatic example occurred in 2004 when some two hundred incensed women attacked a local rapist and thug, Akku Yadav, in the least likely of places: inside a courtroom. They threw chilli powder into his face, cut off his penis and took turns to stab him to death. The officers guarding him fled in terror.

Yadav and his gang had been terrorizing lower-caste Dalit families in their slum neighbourhood for years, extorting money, murdering and raping. Complaints to the police went unanswered or were turned back on the complainant. The local police, well bribed, were in cahoots with Yadav and informed him when someone had accused him. He would then go after them. But word got round that a woman in the village had finally stood up to him, which emboldened other women. Fearing for his safety, Yadav sought protection from the police. Meanwhile, the district deputy commissioner of police had been persuaded that Yadav should finally be brought to justice and, on the day of his hearing, Yadav was met at the court by a wary group of his victims. Unfazed, he swore retribution on them all and, to the smirks of police officers, taunted one of his rape victims. She was furious and cursed him loudly, which served as a signal to the women present: the revenge rampage began. Some arrests were made afterwards, but following mass protests and 'arrest us all' cries from the women of the village, the detainees were released.[10]

Other incidents followed. In 2008 a village woman in the state of Uttar Pradesh was cutting grass with a sickle when she was sexually attacked from behind by a man who had been harassing her for months. In a 'bid to save her dignity' she swung her sickle and beheaded him, then paraded his bloody head through the village. Charged with culpable homicide, she told police that she had no regrets. And in 2014 an enraged mob of women in Kerala exacted revenge on two local rapists. They stripped them, tied them to railings and beat them for two hours before handing them over to the police.[11] Press coverage of such events, and reports of the violent rape of women in the streets, have helped to raise the profile of women's oppression in India and push the issue further up the political agenda.

GRUDGE STALKING entered the revenge vocabulary in the 1990s with a celebrity tag, the murder of a successful young American actress, Rebecca Schaeffer. She was killed by a sexually obsessed fan who had trailed her for three years. He was incensed at her 'immoral behaviour' after seeing her in a feature movie in bed with a male actor. He followed her to her home and shot her dead when she opened her front door.

Her killing exposed the tip of an iceberg: people persistently pursued by a stranger, or someone they knew. Recent (2014) statistics record 7.5 million stalking cases a year in the USA and 5 million in the UK.[12] Stalkers will trail their target relentlessly and make threatening phone calls, and can appear suddenly at their home or workplace. Their doggedness to track their quarry for months or years marks them apart from one-off harassers. Their motives vary but, according to Paul Mullen of Monash University, grudges are common, and some will not stop until their target is destroyed. The majority of women murdered by their current or former partner have been stalked in the lead-up period.[13]

There are professionals vulnerable to revenge stalking. Up to 50 per cent of surgeons, psychiatrists and psychologists report that they have been stalked by patients, angry about the service they have received or resentful that the relationship has ended.[14] Lawyers, too, have found themselves pursued by aggrieved clients and adversaries, especially ex-husbands angry that an outcome has been unfavourable to them: 'The worst fact, in my opinion, was to see him at night near my home,' said one lawyer. Another spoke of his dread when the threats were extended to his family.[15] Politicians are easy targets. More than half the Members of Parliament in the UK and New Zealand report that they have been intimidated by stalkers: 'Smashed my back door, threw a bullet through my toilet window', 'Death threats, threats of GBH, camera drone photography of house, rubbish bins rifled, verbal abuse . . .'[16] Former Congressman Bob Krueger in the USA was an early casualty. He lost his bid for the U.S. Senate in 1984 and had to disband his campaign staff, including Tom Humphrey, the pilot hired to fly him around for campaign appearances. Humphrey was well liked and reliable, but as others went on their way, he took the dismissal personally. He began bombarding the

Kruegers with phone calls. 'He became obsessed,' said Krueger's wife. 'He would regularly fill up a whole hour-long tape during the night which meant that he had dialled 120 times in a row... I was standing at the stove trying to stir a pot of food and just sobbing because I was so afraid.' Christmas 1987 was a turning point, marked by a message to Bob Krueger: 'I'm going to kill you. I'm going to kill you. I'm going to kill you. I've hired a killer to put a .22-caliber to your head while you lie sleeping next to your wife. You won't be much of an ambassador with a hole in your head.' Tom Humphrey was arrested and imprisoned for a year, but on release the death threats continued, so he was returned to prison. The whole cycle then repeated itself. The Kruegers were left in constant fear.[17] Humphrey's recidivism reflects a common pattern among stalkers – neither imprisonment nor restraining orders stops them; the compulsion is simply too great. They are often troubled individuals: some are mentally ill, others extremely narcissistic.[18] Victims can feel helpless, fearful that the authorities will not take them seriously, or blame them for bringing it on themselves.[19] Some will try to reason with their stalker, or hope that they will eventually give up. These approaches rarely work.

The revenge stalker's options have expanded vastly with the Internet, so much so that cyberstalking is poised to outpace physical stalking.[20] Cyberstalkers have to hand a host of gateways through which to track and attack a victim – websites, emails, blogs, social media and spyware – all enabled by the exponential growth in smartphones and tablets, particularly among adolescents.[21] It is estimated that 20 to 40 per cent of Internet users are victimized, mostly females but a growing proportion of men.[22] Insofar as there are 'typical' cyberstalkers, they are most likely to be male, isolated, in their teens or twenties, anxious or stressed and fixated on Internet life.[23] They are adept at exploiting computer systems to target their victims, enjoying the feeling of control as they anonymously channel their fantasies and hate online. Revenge porn is now one of their main weapons.

Aimed mostly at ex-partners, intimate sexual images are uploaded to hurt or embarrass them and posted to those close to the victim – family, friends, an employer – or, for wider impact, to social networks and revenge porn sites. There are an estimated 3,000 websites hosting revenge porn. Some prohibit publication of the victim's personal information, others encourage it, including name, address, email or Facebook account.[24] Once an image is online it can be very difficult to remove, links spreading virally across virtual domains – being potentially devastating for victims:

> I loved and trusted him, and taking nude photographs and videos was an enjoyable part of our lovemaking. The phrase 'revenge porn' trivialises what felt to me like rape. My life was consumed with contacting websites, trying to get them to take down the video, which they would, but it soon popped up again elsewhere.[25]

Victims report depression, sleeplessness and social withdrawal. Consider Chrissy Chambers. More than a year after a difficult breakup with her partner she was distraught to discover that explicit videos of her had been posted online and shared on dozens of pornography sites: 'I collapsed and broke down in tears . . . I fell into a deep depression. I was diagnosed with post traumatic disorder. I became an alcoholic at the age of 22.'[26] On the day she suggested to her partner that they should part, she remembers getting very drunk, but had no memory of what happened next. In fact, he had sexually assaulted her while she was unconscious, and filmed it. She was alerted to the film's existence by posts on her YouTube channel, criticizing her for 'what she had done'.[27]

The threat of revenge porn has been used to coerce women to remain in abusive relationships, as leverage in custody battles and as 'sextortion': pay up or the images will be released.[28] Revenge porn can blight a victim's career because many employers will now, as a matter of course, research job applicants on the Internet for relevant information, and 'unsuitable' photos and videos are high on their list of reasons to reject a candidate.[29] Behind revenge porn is a vibrant web porn industry, itself an extension of the ancient practice of objectifying women's bodies for male pleasure. The demand appears insatiable. It is estimated that 35 per cent of all Internet downloads are pornographic, with 40 million Americans regularly visiting porn sites.[30] In the UK there are an estimated 1.3 million people dependent on pornography for their sexual arousal, and for whom cybersex has displaced partnered sex.[31]

Under a shield of anonymity a porn viewer can feel invulnerable, 'deindividuated', submerged in an amorphous cyber community and immune to the usual sanctions or moral constraints.[32] Initially, images may be exchanged among people with no particular ill will towards the subject, but communications can deteriorate rapidly as viewers compete with one another on abusiveness and cruelty.[33] A study of Twitter in 2016 revealed that, in a three-week period, 6,500 people were targeted by 10,000 users with sexually aggressive, misogynistic tweets.[34]

Revenge porn is also profitable – from advertisements and fees for 'exclusive' images. One of the first sites, IsAnyoneUp, was run by Hunter Moore in 2010. At its peak it attracted some 35,000 submissions a week and reputedly boosted Moore's income to the tune of $30,000 a month.[35] Uploaders could include the subject's name, profession, social media profile and city of residence, a veritable paradise for avengers and stalkers. Desperate victims would plead with Moore to take down their images, to receive no response or an email, 'LOL'. Other revenge porn site owners took victims' distress as a golden opportunity to earn more money by offering to remove the images for a fee. Craig Brittain, of the website IsAnybodyDown, created a fictitious 'attorney' (himself) who would remove the offensive images for $250. Another owner, Kevin Bollaert, followed in his footsteps. When victims asked him to remove their images from his UGotPosted.com, they were directed to another, ostensibly independent, site, ChangeMyReputation.com. It was run by Bollaert. For several hundred dollars it would remove the images.

Many revenge porn victims feel too ashamed or embarrassed to speak out, and some fear further intimidation if they do. Complaints to the police can appear daunting as they demand detailed evidence, such as screenshots of intimate images, and the times and dates of messages. Indeed, criminalizing revenge porn has been a slow process, entangled in the right to free speech on the web and the protection that the USA grants to web administrators and site visitors from what others post on the site. Nevertheless, there have been some positive moves. In 2016, 34 states in the USA adopted their own bans on non-consensual pornography, and laws against revenge porn were in place in Canada, Israel, Germany, France, Australia and the United Kingdom. In the first year of the UK's ban, more than 1,000 incidents of revenge porn were reported to the police, some from victims as young as eleven. Offences carried a maximum sentence of two-year imprisonment. The European Union's 'right to be forgotten' ruling in 2014 has also helped, a requirement that search engines remove links that contain information that is clearly not in the public interest and infringe an individual's private rights. This has begun to make the Internet a less hospitable place for revenge porn. Other 'causes' are sub-cultural, particularly the adolescent fashion for sexting. A *New York Times* report captures the dark side of the practice:

> One day last winter Margarite posed naked before her bathroom mirror, held up her cell phone and took a picture. Then she sent the full-length frontal photo to Isaiah, her new boyfriend. Both were in eighth grade. They broke up soon after. A few weeks later, Isaiah forwarded the photo to another eighth-grade girl, once a friend of Margarite's. Around 11 o'clock at night, that girl slapped a text message on it: 'Ho Alert!' she typed. 'If you think this girl is a whore, then text this to all your friends' . . . In less than 24 hours . . . hundreds, possibly thousands, of students had received her photo and forwarded it.[36]

For boys, collecting and exchanging sexts is a form of currency and masculine bravado, 'a marketplace, where boys are the consumers and girls are the products to be consumed'.[37] Posting the images online with offensive tags such as 'sluts', 'slags' or 'skets' enhances the boy's prestige amongst his peers, fuelling misogyny.[38] Combatting sexting norms requires persuasive, school-based programmes that stress the damage they can wittingly or unwittingly cause: 'How would you feel if you were a victim?'

YOU PEOPLE ruined my whole life, don't expect me to show mercy today. No one disrespects me and gets away with it. I'll teach you people a little lesson on respect with my 9mm jacketed hollow points. It's time for extreme civil disobedience. Fantasy will become reality today for sure. Where the mind goes the body will follow and, yes, people will die, there's no question about that.[39]

THESE WERE the troubling words found on nineteen-year-old Liam Lyburd's computer. Lyburd's grudge was against Newcastle College in northeast England, for expelling him for 'shocking behaviour' in 2012. His was no idle threat. In his bedroom he had amassed an armoury of pipe bombs, a Glock pistol and ammunition. His laptop contained images of him dressed in combat gear and posing menacingly with a gun. On Facebook he bragged about his intention to massacre students, praising American high school shooters and Anders Breivik, the Norwegian mass murderer. Over a period of two years his revenge fantasies gelled into a plan of action, but they were thwarted at the last moment by the police, alerted to his online posts.

Lyburd's story is prototypical. Since the early twentieth century there have been some ninety rampage attacks in schools and colleges worldwide, taking nine hundred young lives and leaving many more wounded.[40] The USA has been most affected, but Germany, Canada, China, Russia, Israel and Finland have all suffered. Rampage killings are typically unselective, aimed at a group of students or educational institution. For instance, in 2001 fifteen-year-old Charles Williams fulfilled his pledge to 'pull a Columbine' at Santana High School, California, because of the people who had, he claimed, bullied him there. Firing indiscriminately, he wounded thirteen students and killed two. In 2002 nineteen-year-old Robert Steinhäuser returned to the school that had expelled him in the German city of Erfurt, brandishing a shotgun and pistol. He killed thirteen teachers, two students and a policeman. His last words were, 'that's enough for today.' He then killed himself.

Why do these events occur? What, if anything, links them? We know that shooters are predominantly male and see themselves as misfits or marginalized. Some have experienced chaotic parenting or an abusive home life, and a few have had a history of psychopathology. At school or college many have been on the receiving end of homophobic taunts, or mocked by their peers as 'losers', 'nerds', 'geeks' or 'wannabes'.[41] Before they killed twelve students and a teacher in 1999 at Columbine High School in Littleton, Colorado, teenagers Eric Harris and Dylan Klebold were frequently bullied by school athletes ('jocks') and derided for being 'faggots'. 'Everyone is always making fun of me because of how I look, how fucking weak I am,' wrote Harris in his diary. 'Well, I will get you all back: ultimate fucking revenge here.' And as Klebold burst into the school library he screamed, 'Everybody with white hats [jocks] stand up! This is for all the shit you've given us for the past four years!'

In the lead-up, shooters typically retreat into a fantasy world of violent movies and video games. Sensational media reports of rampage killings are inspirational, a model of what they can to do address their pain, hate and injustice – down to the exact weapons and ubiquitous trench coat. The longing to be noticed, to appear powerful, is crucial: 'The more people you kill, the more you're in the limelight,' blogged Chris Harper-Mercer before killing ten people at Umpqua Community College, Oregon, in 2015. Months before wounding 37 people in his former school in Emsdetten, Germany, eighteen-year-old Sebastian Bosse wrote in his diary,

Shit! I feel as if I'm about to croak! My heart hurts so terribly, that I am bent over because of the pain . . . Imagine you are in your old school, imagine the trench coat covers all your tools for justice, and then you throw the first Molotov cocktail, the first bomb. You are sending your most hated place to hell!

In response, schools and colleges in parts of the u.s. have fortified their buildings. Armed guards, metal detectors and surveillance cameras greet students, a forlorn symbol of twenty-first-century education. A major challenge is to spot and defuse the conditions that lead to rampage killings, and interviews with convicted school shooters in the u.s. give us some clues how, like the boy who killed students in Pearl, Mississippi, in 1997, when he was a teenager:

Q. Did any grown-up know how much hate you had in you?
A. No.
Q. What would it have taken for a grown-up to know?
A. Pay attention. Just sit down and talk with me.
Q. What advice do you have for adults?
A. I think they should try to bond more with their students . . . Talk to them . . . It doesn't have to be about anything. Just have some kind of relationship with them.
Q. And how would you have responded?
A. Well, it would have took some time before I'd opened up. If we kept talking . . . I would have . . . said everything that was going on.[42]

There is a role here for teachers, school counsellors and parents to be alert to warning signs, such as psychological withdrawal. Parents are wont to dismiss their teenager's withdrawal as 'just a teenage thing', and indeed, that was how Dylan Klebold's mother reacted before he became one of the killers of the Columbine High School massacre. She described how her son had shown outward signs of depression, but neither she nor her husband was able to decode what it meant.[43]

In the final analysis, rampage shootings thrive on guns, and the more straightforward they are to obtain the easier it is to turn revenge fantasies into the real thing. The U.S. Secret Service analysed 37 school shootings to conclude that getting weapons was not difficult: 'Most attackers were able to take guns from their homes or friends, buy them (legally or illegally), or steal them. Some received them as gifts from parents.'[44] When a troubled youth is part of a wider 'guns solve problems' culture, their way forward is fairly clear. Rampage killings are rare or unknown in countries with strict gun laws. Japan has some of the most stringent controls, with just six deaths from guns in 2014 compared to more than 33,000 in the U.S.[45] Only one school rampage killing has been recorded in Japan. America's entrenched gun ownership ensures that, for the foreseeable future, youths bent on revenge will always find the deadly weapons with which to achieve their aims.

SEVEN

VENGEANCE
IN WAR

'Righteous revenge' is potent rhetoric for going to war. It is also unremittingly self-reinforcing. France entered the First World War partly to avenge its defeat and land-grab by Germany during the Franco-Prussian War. Twenty-six years later Hitler reversed the position once more with his occupation of Paris, delivering on his promise to the German people to avenge their humiliation in the First World War. The shock following the bombing of Pearl Harbor in 1941 prompted President Roosevelt to proclaim it 'a date which will live in infamy' and he instructed a revenge attack on Tokyo. Meanwhile Hitler was preparing his v-1 missiles ('v' for *Vergeltungswaffen*, 'retaliatory weapons') for attacks on London, which triggered retaliatory carpet-bombing of German cities. More recently Al-Qaeda declared the destruction of the World Trade Center as revenge against the u.s. and the West in defence of Islam, which in turn inspired the American-led 'war on terror' that would, according to President George W. Bush in 2001, 'bring justice to our enemies'. Attacks and counter-attacks continue to this day.

Civil wars can unleash historic feuds, straining a nation's capacity to contain deadly score-settling. For example, early in Rwanda's history the Tutsis were considered an elite minority of cattle herders compared to the lower status Hutus who farmed the land. It set the seal on a long and unequal division of power between them. 'Smarter' Tutsis were favoured by Rwanda's German colonizers in the nineteenth century, a difference perpetuated by the Belgian colonizers who followed them, who enforced a divide-and-rule policy. In the 1950s the Hutus began to resist the decades of oppression and Tutsi dominance, leading to sporadic armed attacks, counterattacks and vendettas. The tension exploded in the 1990s in one of the fastest and most efficient killings in history: 800,000 Tutsis slaughtered in just one hundred days. There were parallels in Nigeria. In the 1960s a bloody civil war broke out in Nigeria's southern provinces between rival tribal communities, divided by values, customs and political systems. Coup and counter-coup marked the vicious conflict for control, with widespread reprisals unleashed on the Igbo tribe in particular. It is estimated that some two million civilians died of starvation along with 100,000 military casualties.

Vengeance often peaks in the final throes of a conflict. In ancient times, before war crimes were thought of, pillaging a besieged town or city and slaughtering its citizens was no less than what a conquered people deserved. The Vandals were of this mindset when they plundered Rome, the Crusaders when they ransacked Jerusalem and the Ottoman Turks when they looted Constantinople – a 'harrowing and terrible' time, according to a contemporary chronicler: 'Enraged Turkish soldiers . . . gave no quarter . . . they were intent on pillage and roamed through the town stealing, disrobing, pillaging, killing, raping, taking captive men, women, children, old men, young men, monks, priests, people of all sorts and conditions.'[1] Eight hundred years later this practice has resurfaced in Isis's torture, beheading, crucifixion or enslavement of the 'enemies of Islam' in territories it has forcefully occupied. Any captive who does not share their fundamentalism has been marked out for destruction, including Shia Muslims, the 'apostates' who 'must die in order to forge a pure form of Islam'.[2]

Abortive coups and failed uprisings often end in an orgy of revenge. In Africa there were 170 coup attempts between 1956 and 2001; more than half of them failed, leading to immediate revenge purges.[3] Fearing for their lives, coup leaders would often go into hiding or seek sanctuary in a sympathetic country. Typically, those caught faced imprisonment, torture or execution. After the ending of the rebel uprising in Syria in 2016, government revenge squads were reportedly scouring the flow of refugees for suspected rebels and murdering them.[4] Also that year, a faction of Turkey's armed forces attempted to overthrow President Erdogan, supposedly in defence of the country's secular traditions in the face of Erdogan's Islamization. They failed. In a draconian 'cleansing', and amid calls for the restoration of capital punishment, Erdogan ordered the arrest and internment of some 9,000 people – generals, admirals and soldiers. Thousands more were dismissed or removed from their posts, including judges, police officers, teachers, professors, clerics and intelligence officials.

AN END to war is not the end of suffering for victims of war crimes. War criminals should be held legally to account, but in post-war confusion it can be difficult or impossible. Clandestine state-sponsored 'justice' is a controversial, if morally defensible, alternative. Israel travelled this path after the Second World War, assigning Mossad, its specialist intelligence unit, to track down Nazi war criminals who had escaped justice. Assassination was viewed as righteous revenge on particular Nazis, such as Herbert Cukurs, the 'Butcher of Riga'. Cukurs was directly implicated in the murder of 30,000 Latvian Jews, many at his own hand. Mossad agents managed to ensnare him in an elaborate trap in Uruguay, where he was in hiding. They shot him and left his corpse in a trunk with a note listing his crimes, and signed 'We Can Never Forget'.

Adolf Eichmann was an even more important target for Israel. He was the key SS official in charge of deporting European Jewry to the concentration camps, and had evaded capture by escaping to Argentina (aided by former SS comrades). Israel did not want him assassinated, but put on public trial, a vital symbolic event. In an elaborate plan, Mossad kidnapped him and smuggled him out of the country aboard a plane. Unlike Cukars, Eichmann had not personally killed anyone, but he had fully embraced the Nazi doctrine and was responsible for the appalling conditions on the transport trains. His conduct provoked philosopher Hannah Arendt, present at his trial in Jerusalem, to speak of the 'banality of evil'; heinous acts made possible by unreflective bureaucrats who are 'just doing their jobs'. They are desk killers. He was convicted of crimes against humanity and sentenced to death. But should he have died, given, he claimed, he was 'just following orders' and did not, himself, feel guilty?[5] Arendt, reflecting on the verdict, concluded thus:

> And just as you [Eichmann] supported and carried out a policy of not wanting to share the earth with the Jewish people and the people of a number of other nations – as though you and your superiors had any right to determine who should and who should not inhabit the world – we find that no one, that is, no member of the human race, can be expected to want to share the earth with you. This is the reason, and the only reason, you must hang.[6]

The end of a brutal dictatorship can release an intense desire for retribution and justice from those who have suffered at its hands. Yet these legitimate feelings are often sidelined by nervous new governments, striving to avoid a backlash from previous regime supporters as they consolidate their rule. Franco, for example, crushed his political and ideological enemies by execution, forced labour, concentration camps and torture, but two years after his death Spain instituted an amnesty law to help smooth the transition to democracy. It effectively blocked justice for surviving victims like José Galante. As a young, left-leaning college student he was arrested by Franco's police, taken to a basement torture chamber, handcuffed to the ceiling, taunted and repeatedly kicked and beaten in the face and chest. In 2014 he was startled to discover his torturer alive and well nearby. 'I agree with the idea of reconciliation,' Galante reflected, 'but you just can't turn the page. You have to read that page before you turn it.'

In 1988, after fifteen years in power, Augusto Pinochet, military ruler of Chile, read the runes and issued a decree that protected him and his henchman from prosecution. He had overthrown an elected government, murdered an estimated 3,200 people and tortured 28,000 of his political opponents. His 'caravan of death' flew by helicopter to different garrisons across Chile, executing some ninety detainees held in army custody. Following his downfall, his amnesty decree lived on, protected by Chile's powerful conservatives. Pinochet died in 2006, never convicted for human rights abuses. In 2014, on the 41st anniversary of the coup, the socialist President Michelle Bachelet finally spoke of nullifying the amnesty law: 'Witnesses, survivors and victims who saved their own lives are now elderly people. Many of them have died waiting for justice. Many have died in silence. We've had enough of painful waiting and unjustified silences.'[7] Since then hundreds of cases have been sent to prosecutors, a cause for much joy for Veronica de Negri, whose nineteen-year-old son was burned to death by Chilean soldiers during the dictatorship for photographing a political protest. The amnesty laws had thwarted her previous attempts to obtain justice, but now seven former military officers were charged: 'I wanted to scream to the world what was happening,' she said.[8]

Another illustration is Argentina's junta in the 1970s. It overthrew the rule of Isabel Peron and began its Dirty War on 'political subversives', anyone associated with socialism. In its seven turbulent years, 30,000 people were killed and 13,000 'disappeared'. One monstrous method was to drug captives and throw them from an aircraft over the Atlantic Ocean. Without dead bodies the junta could deny all knowledge of their fate. Initial attempts by the new Argentinian democracy to bring the perpetrators to justice were foiled by a violent backlash from the military. To appease the military, new laws were rushed through to limit the time for a prosecution and grant immunity to all but top commanders. But eventually, in 2005, the Argentinian Supreme Court struck down the amnesty laws. In 2012 a landmark trial of suspects began, resulting in 250 convictions, including 'death flight' pilots and high-profile members of the junta.

SINCE THE 1990s there have been attempts to heal the wounds of war through restorative rather than punitive justice. In truth and reconciliation commissions, perpetrators and victims are helped towards a mutual understanding. The format was pioneered in post-apartheid South Africa and applied in other post-conflict zones, such as Sierra Leone, Peru, Guatemala, Morocco, Liberia, the Solomon Islands and Colombia. A victim and perpetrator can come together under the auspices of a 'worthy' independent chairperson to describe in detail what happened to them: the victim on what they suffered at the perpetrator's hands, the perpetrator on their feelings about what they have done. At best this creates space for mutual appreciation, remorse and perhaps forgiveness. Restorative justice is invariably emotionally charged and requires moral courage from both victim and perpetrator.

Some conflicts are historically so entrenched that they appear beyond the reach of any justice, let alone one that is restorative. Vamuk Volkan, professor of psychiatry at the University of Virginia, speaks of a 'chosen trauma' transmitted across generations.[9] The notion captures the sufferings and humiliations of a people that are embedded in their collective identity. Examples include the Crusades for Arab Muslims, the Holocaust for Israelis, the Israeli occupation for Palestinians, the British occupation of Las Malvinas for Argentinians, the ancient Battle of Kosovo for the Serbs, the Turkish invasion for Greek Cypriots and the Turkish genocide for Armenians. The trauma validates their victimhood and heightens any existential threat, justifying, in their eyes, revenge on their enemies and their enemies' descendants.

Take the long conflict between Israel and Palestine. The Holocaust was a crisis of cataclysmic proportions for Jews, obliterating a third of the world's Jewish population and causing unfathomable loss and grief. For Jews, the creation of the State of Israel in 1948 marked the beginning of a permanent security. After centuries of persecution, 'never again' would Jews be hunted, haunted and degraded. Israel would be the safe and rightful home for Jews of various creeds and persuasions, united under Zionism's liberal socialist banner. Realizing this vison has been costly. In Israel's seven decades of existence it has fought eight recognized wars, two Palestinian intifadas, and a series of armed conflicts and revenge operations. Hostile Palestinians and belligerent neighbouring states are a constant reminder of Israel's existential vulnerability and Israel's children are imbued with the belief that Palestinians will be their enemies for ever.[10] Passivity, though, is out of the question given the terrible price paid in the past. So massive walls, watchtowers, overwhelming force and reprisals have become a familiar feature of daily life in Israel.

Tellingly, Palestinians call the creation of the Jewish State the 'nakba' or 'catastrophe'. As they see it, they were expelled from their homeland and left stateless. Many fled to nearby Gaza, and others (some 1.5 million) became permanent residents of refugee camps scattered across Jordan, Lebanon, Syria, the West Bank and East Jerusalem. Successive defeats by Israel have deepened Palestinians' sense of loss, humiliation and shame. In the political stalemate, revenge attacks on Israel, small and large, restore some sense of honour and reinforce a Palestinian identity. The message is passed down generations, children well versed in the language of martyrdom against an implacable enemy. 'Today, the symbol of power is the martyr,' says Eyad El Sarraj, a Palestinian psychiatrist and human rights campaigner. 'If you ask a child in Gaza today what he wants to be when he grows up, he doesn't say that he wants to be a doctor or a soldier or an engineer. He says he wants to be a martyr.' There is no shortage of volunteers for suicide missions:

> You don't need schools for that. All you need is to see Israeli soldiers humiliating your father or Phantom-16s destroying your homes, and the message gets through. Hamas doesn't need to recruit. One of my colleagues told me about a patient who became very depressed when he

was passed over as a suicide bomber; he had missed his chance to be a martyr.[11]

Numerous checkpoints assert Israel's power over the Palestinians. Human rights lawyer Michael Croydon describes what he has witnessed:

Palestinians must stop their cars, hand over their ID documents, and submit to questioning as to where they intend to go, what they do for a living etc. They must also disembark their vehicle and open the boot for Israeli soldiers. Young Israeli conscripts rudely bark orders to Palestinians in Hebrew, the unsaid assumption being that the subjugated people must speak the language of the oppressor. Fathers are treated with disrespect in front of their children, causing untold damage to their authority at home.[12]

The proliferation of Israeli settlements on Palestinian land rubs salt into the wound. 'Every time a Palestinian villager looks out of his window', continues Croydon, 'he sees the settlement on the top of the hill – the dominating Lord of the Land, master of all he surveys ... It is this daily, constant humiliation that is the essence of the Palestinian experience.' Between major uprisings, intifadas, Palestinian resistance is splintered. Stoning and stabbing Israeli soldiers and citizens have become regular, almost ritualistic, expressions of anger and revenge, normally met with tear gas or lethal force. Rocket attacks, hit-and-run incursions and suicide bombings inflict deeper wounds on Israel and lead to more extreme counter-attacks. Israel, unlike Palestine, channels its reprisals through a strong centralized authority and a sophisticated military apparatus, although vigilante incidents have increased in recent years.[13]

Here is a bitter conflict between military unequals, each wedded to historical traumas that define their respective positions, victimhood and hypersensitivity to events around them. Physical and psychological barriers sustain the status quo and feed mutual vengefulness. So far, third-party interventions have failed to bridge the yawning gulf, complicated by the partisan alliances among world powers. But it is vital to keep trying.

WAR AND compassion do not mix well. A nineteenth-century Swiss businessman, Henry Dunant, was troubled by this. He was a man of religious and humanitarian persuasion who, in 1859, witnessed one of the bloodiest battles of the nineteenth century in the northern Italian town of Solferino. The battle was decisive in the struggle for Italian unification and led to more than 40,000 killed or left injured without adequate medical care, with men dying from simple wounds. Dunant recorded what he saw:

> When the sun came up . . . it disclosed the most dreadful sights imaginable. Bodies of men and horses covered the battlefield; corpses were strewn over roads, ditches, ravines, thickets and fields; the approaches to Solferino were literally thick with dead; here and there were pools of blood . . . Some who had gaping wounds already beginning to show infection were almost crazed with suffering. They begged to be put out of their misery, and writhed with faces distorted in the grip of the death struggle.[14]

Dunant proposed international relief societies that could care for the wounded on the battlefield, an idea that attracted the attention of the Geneva Society of Public Welfare. In 1863 the Society appointed Dunant to a small committee to explore how his plans could be put into practice. It marked the birth of the Red Cross. Dunant used his money and good offices to persuade nations to join up, and many did at a landmark conference in Geneva in 1864. The Geneva Convention (to become Geneva Conventions after successive treaties) prescribed the humanitarian obligations of warring states: to care for casualties and prisoners of war and protect civilians and innocent bystanders.

The major wars of the last 150 years have been brutal and devastating but, arguably, they would have been more so without the Geneva Conventions and the rigours of military discipline. However, the picture is very patchy. War progressively dehumanizes and compassion can be an early casualty, evident in the torturing and summary execution of captured enemy fighters and deliberate attacks on civilians. Rape, for instance, is outlawed in most military manuals and codes of battle, but war unleashes dark misogynistic forces. An enemy's women are doubly tainted: they are of the enemy, so they 'deserve' defilement; and being 'weak', 'soft', 'cheap' or ' loose', they are exploitable or expendable. When the Japanese invaded Nanking in 1937, women of all ages were savagely raped and mutilated throughout the city. Japanese military protocol officially prohibited it, but that was easy to get around by destroying the evidence. 'We took it in turns to rape them', confessed a former Japanese soldier, 'but we always stabbed and killed them. Because dead bodies don't talk.' Another added, 'Perhaps when we were raping her we looked on her as a woman, but when we killed her, we just thought of her as something like a pig.'[15] The Rape of Nanking tarnished Japan's military image, so in the Second World War they confined sexual services to 'comfort stations', which provided 'professionalized' sex for deserving troops.[16] In practice, however, it created traumas that resonate today. Women were deceived, bribed or abducted into sexual slavery, and suffered rape, beatings and disease. Most of them died.

Inside Nazi Germany Jewish girls were regularly raped by German soldiers and forced into prostitution. In her book, *Against Our Will*, Susan Brownmiller describes one such incident:

> Forty Jewish girls were dragged into the house which was occupied by German officers. Thereafter being forced to drink, the girls were ordered to undress and to dance for the amusement of their tormentors. Beaten, abused, and raped, the girls were not released until 3 am.[17]

Stalin condoned the rape of German women towards the end of the war. In his eyes it was justified revenge for the 13.5 million Russian deaths at the hands of the Germans.[5] A letter home from a Red Army soldier was upfront about it: 'They do not speak a word of Russian, but that makes it easier. You don't have to persuade them. You just point a revolver and tell them to lie down. Then you do your stuff and go away.'[19] Another was equally blunt: 'And now we take our revenge on the Germans for all their despicable acts committed against us. We're being allowed to do what we please with the German scoundrels.'[20] Rape can be used as a tool of genocide. In Bosnia in the 1990s, raping Muslim women was an obligation and rite of passage for a Serbian soldier, a mark of his ethnic superiority and manhood. Women were raped in their houses, in brothels and in special camps, sometimes repeatedly until pregnancy was confirmed: 'Now you are going to have our children. You are going to have our little Chetniks,' was a regular taunt.[21]

CONVICTIONS FOR wartime rape have been rare. Neither the Tokyo nor Nuremberg war crimes trials brought charges for rape or sexual enslavement. The International Criminal Court, which came into force in 2002, has a mixed record for convictions for sexual crimes. Thomas Lubanga Dyilo, for example, was brought before the court in 2012. According to prosecution witnesses, the repeated rape of girls was a daily occurrence under Dyilo's military command in the Democratic Republic of Congo. Women were tortured and mutilated; boys were trained to rape and use girls as sex slaves. Even though thirty witnesses testified to sexual violence, the prosecutor claimed he could not prove the connection between Dyilo and the killings and rapes. Two years later Germain Katanga stood in the same dock and faced a similar verdict. The militia he commanded in the Congo had mutilated and massacred some two hundred villagers. Female witnesses testified to the traumatic effects of gang rape and forced sexual slavery as 'wives': 'My body was affected. My God, I was very ashamed. Now I have become useless,' confessed one. Katanga was convicted of crimes against humanity, but not of rape and sexual slavery. Both verdicts, Dyilo's and Katanga's, drew sharp criticism from humanitarian organizations and legal analysts. But the legal tide finally began to turn in 2016 with the conviction of Jean-Pierre Bemba, a Congolese politician and military leader. He was sentenced by the court to eighteen years imprisonment for sexually terrorizing the civilian population. Some 77 witnesses and seven hundred documents attested to his central role in sexual abuses.

The Geneva Convention was originally conceived for interstate wars and regular armies. Nowadays there are wars not declared as wars, there are guerrilla wars, civil conflicts involving factional armed groups, terror networks that cross national boundaries and combatants who mingle invisibly with the civilian population. Protagonists are often unmoved by accusations that they have committed war crimes, or that their revenge attacks have killed or injured many civilians. Schools, hospitals and places of worship, once safe havens, have been regularly targeted, transforming grief-stricken civilians into cold-hearted avengers. The red cross sign no longer guarantees protection. In 2013 more than three hundred relief workers were killed or injured worldwide, and more than 140 were kidnapped.[22] Henry Dunant would have turned in his grave.

Stripped of its rhetoric, war is inherently dehumanizing and vengeance freely flows. As psychologist Philip Zimbardo once said, 'the line between good and evil is permeable and almost anyone can be induced to cross it when pressured by situational forces.'[23] This, for Zimbardo, was a major reason why ordinary Germans, people who were not ss ideologues, could be indoctrinated to be enthusiastically cruel.[24] In this light a news story that broke in 2004 shocked the world: graphic images of the torture and appalling humiliation of detainees by u.s. military guards at the Abu Ghraib detention centre in Iraq. An embarrassed u.s. government was keen to put a lid on the episode by blaming 'a few bad apples', but the actual context was more complex. At the time there was widespread fear and panic over the deaths of u.s. soldiers from insurgent violence, which prompted a mass round-up of suspects. Abu Ghraib was flooded with detainees and an intense desire for revenge. Accordingly, Abu Ghraib's cruelties could be seen as less about 'bad apples' and more about a reaction to a toxic environment and collapsed accountability. Or, put differently in the words of ethicist Paul Vallely, 'brutalized men do brutal things . . . war cannot be one soldier's private burden'.[25] The guard or soldier is morally culpable for what they do, but so are the people who put them there.

Another pertinent case looks more clear-cut. Alexander Blackman served as a British Royal Marine in Afghanistan in 2012, during which time his helmet camera recorded him shooting a badly injured Taliban insurgent in the chest at point-blank range. He is heard saying, 'Shuffle off this mortal coil, you cunt. It's nothing you wouldn't do to us.' Then, realizing what he had just done, he turned to his buddies, 'Obviously this doesn't go anywhere, fellas. I just broke the Geneva Convention.' This was more than enough to convince a court martial that Blackman had committed murder in an unwarranted act of revenge. He was sentenced to ten years in prison.

The verdict, however, provoked a sharp public backlash. Was it really murder? More than 30,000 people signed a parliamentary petition that 'a soldier should never go to prison for killing the enemy in a battlefield situation'. Up until then Blackman had an impeccable service record and was focused on his own and his comrades' survival in what was widely dubbed 'the tour from hell'. Insurgents were known to skin their captives alive, behead them and use body parts to lure others into booby traps. Blackman had already lost seven of his comrades and was edgy and exhausted. An appeal court eventually reviewed the verdict and ruled that the original sentence had indeed failed adequately to factor in his combat stress. His conviction was replaced with manslaughter on the grounds of diminished responsibility and his sentence reduced to seven years. He was freed in 2017.

EIGHT

WORK AND
REVENGE

There are some dramatic instances of workplace revenge, such as in the case of Patrick Sherrill. He killed fourteen of his fellow postal workers and injured six others at the post office in Edmond, Oklahoma, in 1986. An ex-marine and sharpshooter, he felt picked on by his supervisors and was angry about being disciplined for his 'erratic behaviour'. He left us with the term 'going postal'.

Much workplace revenge, though, is more subtle, even mundane. The boundaries of tolerance and acceptability are always being tested as we interact with others at work: status, self-esteem and power are on the line. And in the jostle for ascendancy, revenge can often blend invisibly with competition. The corporate careers of Cornelius Vanderbilt of railroad and shipping fame, Lee Iacocca of Chrysler Motors and Steve Jobs of Apple, are said to have been moulded in this vein, each determined to get their own back on people who had previously rejected their ideas, and prove them wrong.

There are formal contracts and psychological contracts, both sources of tension when breached. Psychological contracts are the unspoken understandings when working with one's fellow human beings, such as respecting each other's dignity and not abusing one's position or power. Here, low-level revenge can be a 'feel good' corrective to minor infringements, particularly when status differences inhibit other means, as a British worker admitted:

> After repeated torrents of verbal abuse, I have to confess to, on two occasions, putting laxative in my manager's tea at mid-morning tea break. The result is that she is off for at least the rest of the day (once 2 days) giving me a slight break and affording myself and my colleagues some peace.[1]

In another case a manager's assistant decided to absent himself from work without warning on the very day that he and the manager were to discuss an important report with the CEO. His manager would regularly take the credit for reports that his assistant had written, but today the worm had finally turned. The manager was left speechless and embarrassed in the face of the CEO's probing questions.[2]

Psychological contracts come under strain at times of job loss, and victims often harbour grudges about the way their dismissal has been handled. Some, in revenge, are determined to make their feelings known. Timothy Lloyd, the chief programmer at Omega Engineering, New Jersey, felt this way after he lost his job the 1990s. He contrived to place a virtual 'bomb' inside the company's computer network, which 'exploded' as soon as anyone switched on their computer. It permanently deleted all the company's design and production programs and caused $100,000 of damage. Likewise, Oscar Ramos-Lopez retaliated using insider knowledge when he was fired from a Texas car dealership in 2010. He hacked into the company's special vehicle-disabling technology, remotely incapacitating a hundred cars around the city of Austin. He also transferred some leases to the account of a deceased rapper.[3] Diane

Kuprewicz, too, was imaginative in her revenge. Stung by her dismissal from the School of Visual Arts in New York in 2002, she posted a convincing fictitious advertisement on a website for applications for the post of the school's human resources director (her bête noire). For good measure she also registered him on several pornographic websites.[4]

WORKER SABOTAGE has occupied a special niche in the history of industrial relations. The term is believed to have derived from the wooden clogs, *sabots*, worn by nineteenth-century factory workers in France. They were, goes one view, tossed into the machinery by workers, in protest at the poor working conditions. A rather different perspective is that *sabot* was slang for poor clog-wearing peasants in France who were recruited to strike-break during the Industrial Revolution. As the machinery was unfamiliar to them, the quality of their work suffered, hence *saboter* came to mean 'to bungle a job' and *sabotage* the bodged product. Post-strike, regular workers were delighted to inherit a new bargaining tactic – sabotage.[5] Either way, sabotage soon became associated with deliberate, vengeful damage, spectacularly in the early 1800s when skilled Nottingham weavers, Luddites, wrecked their new weaving frames. On 29 February 1812 a shocked *Leeds Mercury* reported on their activities:

It is with deep regret we have to state that outrages of a most alarming description and extent have been recently committed in the neighbourhood of Huddersfield. On the night of Saturday last, a number of persons assembled near the premises of Mr Joseph Hirst, of Marsh; with their faces blacked, and their persons in other respects disguised, and having forcibly obtained admittance into the dressing shops, proceeded to destroy all the machinery used in the dressing of cloth such as dressing frames, shears, and other implements used in what is commonly called Gig Mills, the whole of which they completely demolished.

Luddite has become synonymous with mindless opposition to technological progress, but that fundamentally misconstrues the Luddites' motives. The weavers' quarrel was not with the machines but with the injustice. Charlotte Bronte captured it well in her 1849 novel *Shirley*:

certain inventions in machinery were introduced into the staple manufactures of the north, which, greatly reducing the number of hands necessary to be employed, threw thousands out of work, and left them without legitimate means of sustaining life ... Misery generates hate. These sufferers hated the machines which they believed took their bread from them; they hated the buildings which contained those machines; they hated the manufacturers who owned those buildings.[6]

Nowadays workplace sabotage takes many different forms, but is often a symptom of ineffective grievance procedures, or of major misunderstandings between workers and management. In the 1970s new fast-paced assembly lines at General Motors' Ohio plant took away much of the satisfaction and control that operators had over their work. In echoes of the Luddites, their frustration boiled over and they damaged the key product – the cars on the line. They also set a fire that shut down the assembly line, resulting in some $40 million in lost production. More recently, the UK construction industry struggled to make sense of an outbreak of thousands of pounds of damage to works in progress, such as slashed laminate flooring, severed control cables and graffiti. The sector was known for its less-than-ideal working conditions and unpredictable work cycles, but something else seemed to have provoked the reaction. It was common practice to recruit agency workers to fill gaps in permanent staff on particular projects, but on higher rates of pay, which left permanent employees feeling as if they were second-class workers.[7]

Minor acts of sabotage can bring relief from intrinsically alienating or monotonous work – by, say, pulling a fire alarm, adding an amusing virus to the company's intranet, or as Toys 'R' Us discovered to its embarrassment in 1990, cross-dressing dolls of Barbie's boyfriend Ken in Barbie's clothes.[8] Worker sabotage has become a feature of the burgeoning service industries, a reaction to abuse from customers prepared to indulge their 'regal' status.[9] Restaurant workers, information clerks, airline workers and call centre operators have been at the centre of such maltreatment. A restaurant worker captures the atmosphere where she works: 'We're robots to respond to their finger clicks. I wouldn't treat a dog, the way they treat us.'[10] Open retaliation could cost them their job, but covert revenge confers a little self-respect: 'I spat in his coffee and watched him drink it up!' Offensive diners have been placed in the worst possible tables, told (falsely) that their credit card has been rejected, and 'accidentally' had food spilt over them. An experienced restaurant worker explains: 'You walk back to your station thinking "yeah, so that showed you . . . I'm just as clever as you . . . just as good as you". You need to do that; otherwise they'd grind you down. You need to score one every now and again just to remind yourself that you're just as good as they are.'[11]

For customers, call centres have become a familiar, if frustrating, way of doing business, while on the other end of the line, the call centre worker is open to all manner of customer abuse. Call centres have been likened to modern-day sweatshops, 'albeit with mildly improved wages and less manual labour', as one critic puts it.[12] Operators are typically instructed to 'not take it personally' when they are abused, and to 'smile down the phone'. Their workplace is characteristically open-plan so they can be observed, their performance tracked and calls periodically monitored. An ex-worker describes how, after ten months, he had to leave because he felt so depressed about the rage he experienced: 'You develop thick skin, but taking abuse all day, every day when you're just trying to do your job gets incredibly draining. You have little to no rights or power. You're put under tremendous pressure to hit targets.'[13] It is hard for the most seasoned of operators to 'not take it personally' when abused by customers, so some retaliate stealthily by putting them on hold for long periods, by deliberately transferring them to the wrong department, or by telling them that their problem has been fixed when it has not.[14]

Airline ground and cabin crew are at the forefront of the 'smile business', an orientation openly celebrated in recruitment drives. 'When you're smiling, the whole world smiles with you', ran an early British Airways job advertisement, and a recent AirAsia one stressed 'inexhaustible smiles' as an 'absolutely essential' requirement for the job. Emirates Air Line has gone a step further in, exhorting passengers to measure their journey 'in smiles', modelled by an image of bright and smiling flight attendants. It is a world of emotional labour, one that seems harmless and joyful, yet in reality can be anything but for the worker.[15] 'You try saying "hello" to three hundred people and sound as though you mean it towards the end', confesses a weary flight attendant. 'Most of us make a game of it. Someone – probably a manager – said "This business is all about interpersonal transactions". He was wrong. It's all about bullshit. If life is a cabaret, this is a bloody circus.'[16]

A flight attendant's day is typically punctuated by delays, compressed schedules and spillage. Passenger abuse and sexualized remarks add to the emotional toll and the urge to retaliate gets harder to resist.[17] But any payback has to be carefully judged: it is not only 'unprofessional', but is often in public view. Cabin crew will regularly collaborate in dealing with unruly travellers by using unofficial, coded signals to warn of lecherous or inebriated passengers, although some are prepared to go further and let their corporate mask slip. In her classic book *The Managed Heart*, Arlie Hochschild tells of the young businessman who asked a flight attendant why she was not smiling. He was startled by her reply: 'I'll tell you what. You smile first, then I'll smile.' The businessman then smiled at her. 'Good,' she replied. 'Now freeze and hold that for fifteen hours.' She then walked away.[18] Another, and rather different practice, has been delicately termed 'crop dusting'. The flight attendant silently breaks wind in the direction of belligerent passengers.[19]

The airline check-in desk is usually the first port of call for the harried passenger and, once more, a testing ground for how a 'happy' desk clerk can deal with any abuse that comes their way. Some, tolerance overstretched, decide to allocate a poor seat to an abuser, or rigidly enforce baggage restrictions. Others use the system more creatively. Sonya's poetic revenge is a noteworthy example:

I thought he'd be happy when I finally got him a commuter flight to his destination. 'For God's sake', he yelled at me, 'what are you a moron? I wouldn't fly in one of those death traps. You must be out of your mind ... Why do they let people like you make decisions?' His last words were, 'If everybody working for this organization is as incompetent as you, no wonder your airline loses money.' He then stormed off. I wished him a good flight as if nothing had happened. The little old lady behind him in line had heard everything, of course, and she sweetly asked how I managed to stay so polite and cheerful in the face of his abusive behavior. I told her the truth. 'He's going to Kansas City,' I explained, 'and his bags are going to Tokyo.' She laughed and told me that I'd done the right thing.[20]

Save the purely malicious, a little revenge at work can go a long way – a modicum of moral recovery and an antidote to inevitable frustrations and injustices. But major employee disruptions suggest a deeper malaise: certainly a failure in systems of consultation or collaboration, possibly more fundamental faults in the nature of the work; all factors that management would be wise not to ignore.

NINE

INSIDE POLITICAL
REVENGE

I n the quest for political power, insults and injuries are not
easily overlooked. Fictional works throughout the ages have
explored this intriguing phenomenon, from Shakespeare to television dramas such as *House of Cards*, *The West Wing* and *Borgen*.
We learn about the price of ambition, about political corruption
and about revenge.

Political revenge in America, said to be as American as apple
pie, was lamented by America's founding fathers. President
John Adams declared it 'the great evil' of political party behaviour: 'There is nothing which I dread so much as a division of the
republic into two great parties, each arranged under its leader,
and concerting measures in opposition to each other.' George
Washington put it more bluntly. In his farewell presidential
speech he warned of 'disorders and miseries [from the] alternate
domination of one faction over another, sharpened by the spirit
of revenge, natural to party dissention'. These words resonate
today as Democrats and Republicans polarize acrimoniously, but
they were tragically prophetic for George Washington's own
chief staff aide, Alexander Hamilton. His political revenge was
personal: a bitter dispute with an opposite party rival, Aaron
Burr, vice president under Thomas Jefferson. He regarded Burr
as an unprincipled rogue, an 'intriguer', out for himself and no

more, and he was not coy about making his views known. Burr, much offended, demanded revenge in the honourable manner of the time: a duel. They met at dawn in New Jersey on 1 July 1804 and discharged their pistols, but it was Burr's bullet that found its mark and Hamilton died of his wounds.[1]

New York in the nineteenth century was in the thrall of the Tammany Society, an exclusive club that was essential for anyone aspiring to political office in the city. Its inner circle was known to be corrupt, yet the Society managed to maintain its grip on the city for around 75 years. When attacked, it would lash out. Following one anti-Tammany campaign, a Tammany official lambasted the critics: 'We want revenge. We want terrible revenge. Such as will satisfy the indignation that we feel over the abuse that was levelled at honest men in official position and for the wrong that was done us ... And it looks now as we will get it!'[2] In an act of reprisal, Tammany blocked a substantial publishing contract with the publisher Harper Brothers for the supply of books to New York schools – because the publisher had refused Tammany demands to sack their *Harper's Weekly* political cartoonist, Thomas Nast. Nast, a keen advocate of political reform, had regularly lampooned Tammany power and the corruption of its boss, William Tweed, who had much of the city under his control. One of Nast's cartoons made the point graphically: an image of a giant Tweed thumb squashing New York City. These cartoons would have had particular impact on Tweed's supporters, many of whom were illiterate. In an attempt to 'stop those damn pictures', Tweed offered Nast a substantial bribe, which he turned down.[3] Tweed was eventually indicted for corruption in 1873. Tammany's fate was sealed fittingly by political revenge at a loftier level: as the Tammany Society refused to back Roosevelt for president in 1932, he officially degraded it when he came to power.

Revenge can be thinly disguised in American domestic politics. Bill Clinton's impeachment for the 'Monica Lewinsky affair' was widely put down to the Republican Party's desire to draw blood, and payback was seemingly behind the Governor of Texas's order in 2004 to audit the state's Comptroller Department, run by Carole Strayhorn, who had long been an outspoken critic of his policies. A political vendetta similarly forced Florida Republican Party chairman Jim Greer from office in 2010. It was, said Greer, because he had backed the 'wrong man' for the Senate: 'Prior to my resignation as chairman, I was told on several occasions that if I didn't stop supporting [him], they would throw the kitchen sink at me and come after me.' They did, and Greer was later convicted for embezzling state funds.[4]

Of all revenge episodes, however, President Nixon's stand apart. The Watergate hearings revealed his party's notorious 'enemies list', drawn up to 'maximize the fact of our incumbency in dealing with persons known to be active in their opposition to our Administration; stated a bit more bluntly – how we can use the available federal machinery to screw our political enemies'. Dozens of political foes, aides and media organizations were on the list, which pulled no punches: 'should be hit hard', 'time to give him the message', 'a scandal here would be most helpful', 'has known weakness for white females'.[5]

Occasionally punches are literally evident on the floor of the legislature, unseemly departures from democracy's verbal duels. Divisive issues can become testosterone-charged and personal. An early u.s. example was the anti-slavery debate in 1860. Republican Owen Lovejoy condemned the Democratic Party's defence of slavery and its racism, which so incensed Democrat

Roger Atkinson Pryor that he came at him with pistols and canes. He had to be dragged off, but not without loud protests from Lovejoy: 'I will stand where I please,' and 'Nobody can intimidate me.'[6] In more recent times, punches were exchanged between Republican Charles Bishop and Democrat Lowell Barron at a session of the Alabama State Senate in 2007. Barron allegedly called Bishop 'a son of a bitch'. Such outbursts have not been confined to the USA; they have surfaced in most democracies at one time or another. Italian members of parliament brawled over pension reforms in 2011, and in 2015 fighting broke out in the Ukrainian parliament after the Prime Minister was pulled from the podium by an aggrieved opposition member. And in that same year, Japan's normally dignified parliament disintegrated into a riot, ironically over a bill to allow troops to fight abroad.

A MALEVOLENT politician or regime has a time-honed weapon at their disposal: character assassination. In the dying days of the Roman Republic, Octavian and Mark Antony were enthusiastic mutual defamers, 'painting each other as either a usurping social upstart or a debauched slave of "oriental" vices, respectively'.[7] 'In the venom of words', according to Martijn Icks and Eric Shiraev, 'a Roman emperor appears as a sadistic maniac. A Byzantine empress is portrayed as an incestuous monster. A top Communist leader is transformed into a cheating renegade, and traitor . . . A female presidential candidate appears as an eerie witch.'[8]

Character attacks are intended to sway opinion against an opponent by undermining their competence, looks, moral probity, health, race, sex life – or anything that might lodge in the public mind and buy political advantage. The smear may be a total fabrication, contain a kernel of truth or be factually accurate, but veracity is beside the point. The political effect is what matters. In the early twentieth century the Communist Party was a major political voice in Germany, but reviled in Nazi propaganda as 'red subhumans'. German Communists were among the first to be sent to the concentration camps. In the 1980s the civic movement Charter 77 challenged the human rights record of Czechoslovakia's Soviet socialism. The regime struck back violently, and through its media channels branded Charter 77 followers as 'agents of international forces', 'contemptuous of the people', 'preoccupied with money and bribery', 'losers and usurpers'.[9] In Burma, democracy champion Aung San Suu Kyi suffered years of intimidation at the hands of the ruling junta, including being mocked in government broadcasts and accused, among other things, of sexual promiscuity.[10]

Character attacks are intense where politics is fiercely personalized, and here America leads the way.[11] Thomas Jefferson, for example, hired a journalist to help him outflank his main opponent, John Adams, in the 1801 presidential race. Up until then their relationship had been amicable; indeed, together they had helped secure America's independence. Party politics, however, had created deep cleavages, and now the gloves were off. One pamphlet described Adams as a 'hideous hermaphroditical character, which has neither the force and firmness of firmness of man, nor the gentleness and sensibility of a woman'. Adams returned the insult, calling Jefferson 'a fool, a hypocrite, a criminal and a tyrant'. The ping-pong of abuse continued throughout the campaign.[12] Some two centuries later, character attacks remain central to American campaigns. In the 2000 Republican presidential primary race, John McCain was accused by his opponents' supporters of being a 'sick war vet', 'married to a drug abuser' and 'father of a black love child'. In Barack Obama's 2004 bid for the Senate, rumours were circulated that he was secretly a Muslim, and in the 2008 presidential campaign an opposition advertisement portrayed him as a dangerous man who was unpatriotic and untrustworthy, associating with financial backers convicted of corruption: 'Who is Barack Obama?'[13]

Political aides and public relations advisers are key players in the smearing process. They are attuned to the intense media interest in political campaigns, secure in the knowledge that unsavoury 'facts' about a politician make far more compelling news than stories about their good works and patriotism. Character attacks capitalize on the human tendency to place greater weight on unfavourable information when making judgements, particularly when it is presented in easily digested sound bites. In 2016 Republican presidential nominee Donald Trump revealed himself to be a master of the genre in scathing personal attacks on his Democratic opponent, Hillary Clinton: 'a world-class liar', 'into personal profit and theft', 'nasty woman', 'should be locked up; I *will* lock her up!', 'callous', 'blood of so many on her hands', 'pretty close to unhinged', 'lacks judgment'.[14] His litany of excoriations dismayed many independent observers, but generally delighted his acolytes.

Do character attacks work? For Trump, who won the presidency against the odds, they seemed to do no harm electorally, and may very well have helped him. The research findings, though, are mixed. Some indicate that, while citizens claim that negative campaigning discourages them from voting, in practice they do the opposite. 'Negative campaigns,' says political scientist Paul Martin, 'may be a kind of guilty pleasure for Americans – they claim to dislike them, but inadvertently are drawn to them in much the same way that shoppers find themselves drawn to the tabloids in the checkout aisle.'[15] Other studies conclude that it is much harder to like and trust a candidate who is intent on demeaning their opponent's character; it fuels voter cynicism.[16] So the jury is out. Meanwhile, there is little indication that character attacks are about to vanish from the American political scene.

PRESS VENDETTAS have long troubled champions of democracy. Two hundred years ago a press-buffeted Thomas Jefferson declared his hand: 'I deplore . . . the putrid state into which the newspapers have passed, and the malignity, the vulgarity and mendacious spirit of those who write them . . . It is however an evil for which there is no remedy; our liberty depends on the freedom of the press, and that cannot be limited without being lost.' In the early twentieth century, the British prime minister Stanley Baldwin was also forthright in his condemnation of the press, rebuking the 'press lords' for using 'direct falsehood, misrepresentation, half-truths, the alteration of the speaker's meaning. What the proprietorship of these papers is aiming at is power, but power without responsibility – the prerogative of the harlot through the ages.'[17]

Domineering press proprietors such as William Randolph Hearst, William Maxwell Aitken and Rupert Murdoch personify the problem. Hearst, the son of a millionaire mine owner, ran a chain of newspapers and magazines across the United States in the late nineteenth and early twentieth centuries, as well as radio stations and movie companies. He pioneered 'yellow journalism' – banner headlines, sensationalized stories and half-truths, the precursor of today's tabloids. Hearst's political agenda surfaced in 1896 in his support of the Democratic presidential candidate, William Jennings Bryan. He approved of Bryan's radical call for silver rather than gold as the currency standard (Hearst's riches were partly from his father's silver mines), but that put Hearst on a collision course with the Republican candidate, William McKinley, who favoured gold. Hearst went out of his way to discredit McKinley in his *New York Journal*, portraying him as an ineffectual man who sucked up to the wealthy business elite, especially to businessman Mark Hanna, McKinley's close aide. A striking *New York Journal* cartoon by Homer Davenport depicted a diminutive McKinley cupped in the controlling hand of Mark Hanna.

McKinley, nevertheless, won the 1896 election with a comfortable majority, fuelling Hearst's determination to discredit him. At the time there were serious revolts in Cuba against Spanish rule, but McKinley, a veteran of the American Civil War, was reluctant to intervene: 'I've been through one war. I have seen the dead piled up, and I do not want to see another.'[18] But his hand was eventually forced by Hearst's war-feverish reporting about Spanish atrocities and his publication of a leaked letter from a Spanish diplomat that described McKinley as a 'weak' and 'petty' politician.

After this intervention Hearst continued to disparage McKinley, angling for the Democratic presidential run himself. An infamous editorial in the *New York Journal* of 10 April 1901 asserted that 'Institutions, like men, will last until they die; and if bad institutions and bad men can be got rid of only by killing, then the killing must be done.' The comment appeared shortly before McKinley was assassinated by an anarchist on 6 September 1901, and some blamed Hearst's inflammatory editorials for inspiring the killer. Hearst made a bid for political office in 1922 as Senate nominee for New York – solid Tammany territory. The Governor of New York initially backed him, but then changed his mind. Hearst never forgave him, and in revenge switched his newspapers' allegiance to the Governor's political opponents.

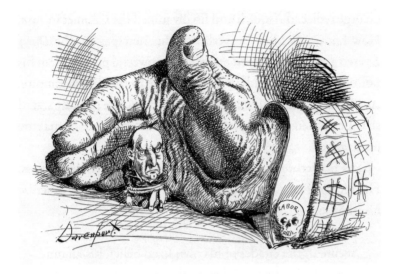

'A Man of Mark', *New York Journal*, 1896.

Compared to Hearst, William Maxwell Aitken's background was comfortable but not gilt-edged. He arrived in London in 1910 from Canada while being investigated by the Canadian authorities for securities fraud, but that did not hamper his career in his adopted country. He was drawn to the world of journalism and politics, and by the end of the year had won a seat in the House of Commons. He gradually increased his stake in the *Daily Express* until he became its outright owner, with a reputation as someone who could make or break prime ministers.

He came to dislike Liberal prime minister Herbert Asquith, partly because of Asquith's growing reputation for mismanaging the war effort during the First World War, and partly because Asquith had not granted him a cabinet post. Aitken retaliated by conspiring to unseat Asquith in 1916, later describing it as an 'honest intrigue' and the 'biggest thing I have ever done . . . If the Asquith government had gone on, the country would have gone down.'[19] He was rewarded with a peerage after David Lloyd

George replaced Asquith and finally joined the Cabinet in 1918. Now known as Lord Beaverbrook, his newspapers, the *Daily Express* and *Evening Standard*, became powerful platforms for his political views, particularly on free trade in the British Empire. At a Royal Commission into the press in 1948 he proudly stated that he owned newspapers purely for the purpose of making propaganda.

As Beaverbrook's career matured, so did his vindictiveness. His biographers, Ann Chisholm and Michael Davie, describe his mindset:

> Secure in the citadel of his own fixed belief, his ammunition locker well stocked with documents and by his own long and formidable memory, his spies everywhere and a marauding force of researchers and reporters on standby, he could humour himself by taking pot shots at his enemies and keep boredom at bay at the same time.[20]

A secret blacklist, which he termed a 'white list', contained the names of people he considered his enemies. Apart from particular politicians, it included celebrities such as Charlie Chaplin, Paul Robeson and Noël Coward. Coward was there, it seemed, because of the 1942 war film *In Which We Serve*, which he co-directed. The film celebrated the exploits of Captain Lord Louis Mountbatten, a man whom Beaverbrook considered 'a murderer' on account of the huge loss of Canadian lives at the Dieppe landings, under Mountbatten's overall command. The film opened with a mock-up of the *Daily Express*, dated 1 September 1939, floating among dockside detritus, its front page claiming: 'No War This Year'. It parodied the real *Daily Express* headline of 30 September 1938: 'The Daily Express declares that Britain will not be involved in a European war this year, or next year either.' How wrong could you be?

Rupert Murdoch's press-baronial status grew from the business he inherited from his father in the 1950s, a major force in Australia's newspaper industry. Murdoch's newsprint and digital empire stretches across five continents, reaching over half the world's population. His political hubris was on full display after the 1992 Conservative Party victory in the UK, his *Sun* newspaper exclaiming, 'It's The Sun Wot Won It'. Murdoch joins an exclusive band of press barons who have been regularly wined and dined by incumbent and prospective prime ministers.

The Murdoch press regularly bares its political teeth. In the 1990s British Labour politician Clare Short, a doughty campaigner, tried to introduce a private member's bill to curb the publication of photographs of topless females, a regular 'page 3' feature of Murdoch's *Sun*. She was responding to growing feminist disquiet about the demeaning objectification of women's bodies. *The Sun* struck back with malice, branding Short as a 'killjoy', 'fat and jealous'. It compared her appearance to 'the back of a bus' and mocked her campaign by superimposing her head on the body of a topless model, to the tag 'mission impossible'. Ten years later *The Sun*'s editor admitted that they may have gone too far.

In his Australian homeland Murdoch owns two-thirds of the metropolitan press, and his News Corp columnists freely push his political agendas. Misogyny resurfaced in his relentless campaign to unseat Julia Gillard, Australia's first female prime minister in 2010. At her appointment, Murdoch is reported to have made it clear to his assembled staff that he could not tolerate her or many of her Labor policies. He wanted regime change.[21] His journalists went to work with zeal, flooding News Corp papers with critical coverage of her policies and character.[22] His paper, *The Australian,* alleged (and then retracted) that she had once benefited from embezzled union funds. It presented Gillard as out of place in the manly world of political leadership and hardly qualified to speak authoritatively on domestic matters, because she had not 'had to make room for the frustrating demands and magnificent responsibilities of caring for little babies, picking up sick children from school, raising teenagers. Not to mention the needs of a husband or partner.'[23] Gillard's leadership of the Labor Party collapsed in 2013, with more than a little help from the Murdoch press.

Kevin Rudd replaced Gillard as Labor leader and prime minster, returning to the post he had held in 2007. His cabinet contained a record number of women, and he was the first Australian prime minister to support same-sex marriage. But Murdoch was displeased. He had his sights set on someone better suited to his political and business interests: Tony Abbott, leader of the opposition Liberal Party (later dubbed 'Rupert Murdoch's crony'). Murdoch's columnists now began their beatification of Abbott, alongside a character assassination of Kevin Rudd. Across Murdoch's outlets, Rudd was presented variously as a 'volatile, nasty man', 'venomous', 'a selfie-addicted, twittering Facebook junkie', a 'fake', 'a narcissist', 'a psychopath', 'callous and manipulative', 'smirks', 'pouts', 'the more you know him, the more you detest him'.[24] The man, it seemed, had no redeeming qualities. In the 2013 national election he was defeated by Abbott.

A free press, as Thomas Jefferson wisely observed, is integral to an open society, vital for holding the powerful to account. The *Washington Post*'s exposure of the Watergate scandal was a stellar example; however, matters are less straightforward when news and related media are concentrated in the hands of a few powerful owners, with no meaningful mechanisms to hold them to account. In the UK, nearly 80 per cent of the press is owned by a small number of non-resident billionaires, while across Europe, obfuscation is prevalent: it is hard for the public to find out who owns the media in all but a minority of countries.[25] Concentration need not, in itself, be a bad thing if news editors are given a genuine free hand and there is a plurality of political thought among them. Some are of this ilk, but many are not, the owner appointing editors in their own partisan image – 'If politicians want my views they should read Sun editorials', said an unabashed Rupert Murdoch at the Leveson Inquiry into press conduct.[26] With privileged access to politicians, owners of such conviction can launch their vendettas with relative impunity – and democracy is ill served.

THERE IS A FINAL forum for political revenge: the memoir. The prospect of obscurity is unsettling for many high-profile politicians, but with a memoir they can burnish their reputation, settle a score or two, and maybe swell their bank balance: advances of up to $8 million are not uncommon for 'brand name' politicians. Memoirs are often rushed into press because public interest wanes rapidly after a politician has left office. They are typically vainglorious compendiums of memories, snippet conversations, diary notes and interviews, assembled with the help of researchers and ghost writers. Asked about his own presidential memoir, *An American Life*, Ronald Reagan famously quipped, 'I hear it's a terrific book! One of these days I'm going to read it myself!'[27]

An engaging early example was that by James, 2nd Earl Waldegrave, published in 1821. Waldegrave was one of the shortest-serving British prime ministers (just four days in 1757, although 'prime minister' was not the designation at the time). Prior to that, he had been Lord of the King's Bedchamber and governor responsible for the education of the Prince of Wales, the future George III. He valued the governorship, but it was a taxing job, caught between George II's aspirations for his grandson and the determination of the prince's mother, the Dowager Princess of Wales, to stop the King interfering. Enter Lord Bute, a known charmer, Eton-educated, handsome and wealthy. He struck up a friendship with the young Prince of Wales and his mother, which served him well: he was given Waldegrave's post as governor. Waldegrave was deeply resentful and took revenge on both Bute and the princess in his memoirs, published after George III's death. He hinted at a sexual liaison between the two and savaged them both with a mix of backhanded compliments and snide remarks. On Bute:

> fine legs, and a theatrical air of great importance. There is an extraordinary appearance of wisdom, both in his look and manner of speaking; for whether the subject be serious or trifling he is equally pompous, slow, and sententious. Not contented with being wise, he would be thought a polite scholar, and a man of great erudition: but has the misfortune never to succeed, except with those who are exceeding ignorant.

And the princess:

> reputed a woman of excellent sense by those who knew her imperfectly; but, in fact was one of those moderate geniuses, who with much natural dissimulation, a civil address, an assenting conversation, and few ideas of their

own, can act with tolerable propriety, as long as they are conducted by wise and prudent counsellors.[28]

Rarely are political memoirs literary gems, but some authors craft their barbs with style. In *The Time of My Life*, Denis Healey, a British Labour Party grandee in the 1960s and '70s, summed up what it was like working with George Brown, then Foreign Secretary: 'when he was good he was very, very good, but when he was bad he was horrid ... the strain of acting as a psychiatric nurse to a patient who was often violent became intolerable.'[29] And in *A Journey*, Tony Blair also damns the unfortunate Gordon Brown, his successor, with faint praise: 'Political calculation, yes. Political feelings, no. Analytical intelligence, absolutely. Emotional intelligence, zero. Gordon is a strange guy.'[30]

Donald Regan was President Ronald Reagan's powerful chief of staff from 1985 to 1987. He arranged most of the details of the President's political life, but regularly clashed with the First Lady, Nancy Reagan, over what she saw as his hunger for power and excessive control over her husband's affairs. His dismissive attitude towards women also disturbed her. To Regan, she was an interfering spouse.

Regan lost his job after the 'Irangate' inquiry on the selling of illegal arms to Iran, in which it was alleged he was implicated. He was convinced he had been unfairly scapegoated and that Nancy Reagan had been behind his demise. He retaliated in his muscular memoir, *For the Record* (1989). In it he portrayed the president as an ineffectual man, assiduously protected by his wife, a woman who would go out of her way to reproach any of the president's detractors.[31] In a carefully aimed shot, he claimed that Nancy Reagan relied on a personal astrologer to steer presidential decisions, a proclivity normally associated with seventeenth-century rulers. His revelations generated more than a little embarrassment in the White House. When, later that year, Nancy Reagan published her own memoir, pointedly titled *My Turn*, she played down, although did not deny, the astrology story. But she then devoted an entire chapter to the faults of Donald Regan, maintaining that he often acted as if he were the president.[32]

Political memoirs interweave self-branding and revenge, although few, perhaps, as transparently as Sarah Palin's. She was the forceful ('a pit bull who wears lipstick', quipped a comedian) and much-reported running mate of John McCain, Republican candidate in the 2008 presidential election. The title of her memoir, *Going Rogue* (2009), mimicked the phrase used against her by exasperated McCain staff after her off-message remarks in the closing days of the campaign. In her memoir, Palin paints herself in unflinchingly positive terms as a remarkably fine human being, God-fearing, authentic and unwavering. That done, she turns on her many adversaries, settling scores with the McCain entourage and the press for, she claims, continuing to hound her after her defeat, including 'shocking character assassinations of those I love'.

Historian David Torrance observes that memoirs have become a rite of passage for politicians, but they end up as '100,000 words on why I was right and all my opponents were wrong'.[33] He has that about right.

EPILOGUE:
NO END TO REVENGE?

Revenge can be close or distant, online or offline, short-term or never-ending. It is always about a grievance and justice, and shaped by circumstances: tribal, domestic, workplace or political. It is to be expected that a victim of a perceived injustice will feel vengeful, the legacy of ancient emotional programming, so it makes little sense to punish ourselves or others for having these feelings. Whether and how we act on them is another matter, and society – culture – pushes and pulls us in different directions.

Revenge, according to some, is futile because it cannot undo the harm done. But that misses the point about where to focus one's feelings of injustice. The family of a murdered relative will say that nothing can bring back their loved one, but that is no reason for making life easy for the murderer. There is an intense desire to balance suffering with suffering. The urge for retribution lies deep within us and seeks ways around the moral and rational constraints we place on it.

Revenge is much maligned, not always fairly. As we have seen, it can expose and adjust social injustices, and can be an important, low-key way to get by when relationships are skewed or oppressive. Revenge also enjoys certain kudos in competitive circles, praiseworthy in business and sport, inspiring losers to fight back and prove their doubters wrong. Yet what concerns us most is revenge out of control. Laws, moral edicts and religious teachings try to tackle this: extolling the prudence of self-control and suppressing one's hate. Forgiveness ranks high among religious circles and is praised by some psychologists. Indeed, there are some remarkable accounts of victims of horrific crimes who forgive their perpetrators and, in doing so, relieve themselves of some of their pain and anger. The injuries are not necessarily forgotten, but they no longer dominate; they can move on.

But a forgiveness ethic can be entrapping, as well as guilt-inducing: 'I simply cannot forgive him for what he's done, and I feel bad about that, but people keep saying I should try.' Unconditional forgiveness – forgiving without genuine remorse from the perpetrator – is a further complication. Alice Miller, a psychoanalyst with extensive clinical experience with victims of abuse, sees unconditional forgiving as 'drawing a curtain across reality so that we cannot see what is taking place behind it', with negative consequences for the individual and society. She cites parental child abuse where the child, with deeply conflicting emotions, is prepared to excuse their parents without understanding the truth behind the abuse, thus impeding their recovery: 'the effort spent on the work of forgiveness leads them away from the truth.'[1]

Some victims are able to circumnavigate both forgiveness and revenge by redirecting their bitterness towards prosocial ends, helping to change the conditions that gave rise to the kind of abuse they had suffered. They join the ranks of moral unforgivers. Paul Stewart was one. In November 2016 he gave the first of what became a series of moving public confessions from professional footballers in the UK who had been repeatedly sexually abused by their coach when they were children. Stewart said he had locked the trauma away for forty years because of the humiliation, and because the coach had threatened to kill his family if he ever told anyone: 'My family, career, success was a way of forgetting. I cannot say that I never had the thought of revenge. But this is not about revenge; it is about getting the message out there'.[2]

Civilization's anti-revenge veneer is ever fallible, particularly when nations spoil for war. And once the vengeance genie is out of the bottle, it seems very hard to put back. We look back at the butchery and revenge killings of medieval sieges and justice with awe and revulsion, but modern conflicts have scaled up the misery, revenge attacks sweeping all in their path. Humanity's crucial challenge remains: to find better ways of bridging the things that divide us, and nurturing the compassion that connects us.

REFERENCES

ONE: THE ROOTS OF REVENGE

1 'Stone-throwing Baboons Wait Three Days for Revenge in Saudi Arabia', www.albawaba.com, 2 December 2000; 'Gorilla Revenge', www.answers.google.com, 28 February 2005.

2 Dario Maestripieri, *Macachiavellian Intelligence: How Rhesus Macaques and Humans Have Conquered the World* (Chicago, IL, 2007); Frans B. M. de Waal and Lesleigh M. Luttrell, 'Mechanisms of Social Reciprocity in Three Primate Species: Symmetrical Relationship Characteristics or Cognition?', *Ethology and Sociobiology*, IX/2 (1988), pp. 101–18; Frans de Waal, *Chimpanzee Politics: Power and Sex Among Apes* (Baltimore, MD, revd edn 2007).

3 Friedrich Nietzsche, *Human, All Too Human*, trans. R. J. Hollingdale (Cambridge, 1996), p. 317.

4 Ulrich Orth, Leo Montada and Andreas Maercker, 'Feelings of Revenge, Retaliation Motive, and Posttraumatic Stress Reactions in Crime Victims', *Journal of Interpersonal Violence*, XXI/2 (2006), pp. 229–43; Barbara Lopes Cardozo, Reinhard Kaiser, Carol A. Gotway and Ferid Agani, 'Mental Health, Social Functioning, and Feelings of Hatred and Revenge of Kosovar Albanians One Year After the War in Kosovo', *Journal of Traumatic Stress*, XVI/4 (2003), pp. 351–60.

5 Jon Ronson, *So You've Been Publicly Shamed* (London, 2015), p. 162.

6 Jane Goldberg, 'Fantasies of Revenge and the Stabilization of the Ego', www.drjanegoldberg.com, October 2013.

7 Karen Horney, 'The Value of Vindictiveness', *American Journal of Psychoanalysis*, VIII/1 (1948), pp. 3–12.

8 Heinz Kohut, 'Thoughts on Narcissism and Narcissistic Rage', *Psychoanalytic Study of the Child*, XXVII/1 (1972), pp. 360–400.

9 Ben Dattner, 'Reflections on Narcissistic Bosses', www.businessweek.com, 23 June 2009.

10 James Fallon, 'The Mind of a Dictator: Exploring the Minds of Psychopaths and Dictators', www.psychologytoday.com, 11 November 2011.

11 American Psychiatric Association, *Diagnostic and Statistical Manual of Mental Disorders*, 4th edn [DSM-IV-TR] (Washington, DC, 2000); Betty Glad, 'Why Tyrants Go Too Far: Malignant Narcissism and Absolute Power', *Political Psychology*, XXIII/1 (2002), pp. 1–2; Salman Akhtar and J. Anderson Thomson, 'Overview: Narcissistic Personality Disorder', *American Journal of Psychiatry*, CXXXIX/1 (1982), pp. 12–16; Mila Goldner-Vukov and Laurie Jo Moore, 'Malignant Narcissism: From Fairy Tales to Harsh Reality', *Psychiatria Danubina*, XXII/3 (2010), pp. 392–405.

12 Rupert Colley, 'Ekaterina Dzhugashvili – Stalin's Mother', www.historyinanhour.com, 5 February 2013.

13 The autocrat's self-adulatory symbols continue to beguile populations in Syria, North Korea, Zimbabwe and Kazakhstan. Long-time President Nazarbayev of Kazakhstan has added his own touch: his handprint in solid gold, located in a room at the top of the highest tower in the country's capital. Visitors can measure their own hand against his, physically touching this symbol of his greatness – flesh turned to gold.

14 Aleksandr Solzhenitsyn, *The Gulag Archipelago, 1918–56: An Experiment in Literary Investigation* (New York, 2003), III, p. 69.

15 Shiva Balaghi, *Saddam Hussein: A Biography* (Westport, CT, 2006), pp. 6–7.

16 Jerrold M. Post, *The Psychological Assessment of Political Leaders: With Profiles of Saddam Hussein and Bill Clinton* (Ann Arbor, MI, 2005), p. 343.

17 Christopher Hitchens, 'Iraq's 1979 Fascist Coup', speech given at the Commonwealth Club, Palo Alto, 1979, available at www.lybio.net; Brian Wingate, *Saddam Hussein* (New York, 2003).

18 Mark Bowden, 'Tales of the Tyrant', *The Atlantic* (May 2002).

TWO: RELIGIOUS VOICES

1 Quoted in Dawn Warren, 'Judaism', www.towardcommonground.org, accessed 16 January 2017.

2 Yerachmiel Fried, 'Eye for an Eye – Ask the Rabbi', www.aish.com, accessed 16 January 2017.

3 Philippe Buc, 'Some Thoughts on the Christian Theology of Violence, Medieval and Modern, from the Middle Ages to

the French Revolution', *Rivista di storia del cristianesimo*, v/1 (2008), pp. 9–28.

4 Mazood Azhar, 'Jaish Threatens "Smashing Blow" in Kashmir', *Press Trust of India*, 14 October 2001.

5 Acharya Buddharakkhita, trans., 'Kakacupama Sutta: The Parable of the Saw', *Access to Insight (Legacy Edition)*, 10 November 2013.

6 'Radical Buddhist Monk Accused of Inciting Riots that Have Killed Hundreds of Muslims', *New York Post*, 21 June 2013.

THREE: WRITING REVENGE

1 See Henry Bacon, *The Fascination of Film Violence* (New York, 2015), p. 18.

2 Robin S. Rosenberg, ed., *Our Superheroes, Ourselves* (Oxford, 2013); Jeph Loess and Tom Morris, 'Heroes and Superheroes', in *Superheroes and Philosophy: Truth, Justice, and the Socratic Way*, ed. Tom Morris and Matt Morris (Chicago, IL, 2005), pp. 11–20.

3 'Captain America 1 – Enemy, Chapter One', *Marvel Knights* (1 June 2002).

4 Katie Cole, 'What Can Wonder Woman Tell Us About American Culture?', https://anthropologygallery.wordpress.com, 3 June 2012.

5 Gloria Steinem, 'Wonder Woman', in *The Superhero Reader*, ed. Charles Hatfield, Jeet Heer and Kent Worcester (Jackson, MS, 2013), pp. 203–10.

6 'Is Wonder Woman Qualified to Be a UN Ambassador?', www.bbc. co.uk, 21 October 2016.

7 Samuel Henry Butcher, ed. and trans., *Aristotle's Theory of Poetry and Fine Art*, 4th edn (London, 1907, repr. as *Aristotle Poetics*, 1951), p. 53.

8 Marguerite A. Tassi, *Women and Revenge in Shakespeare: Gender, Genre, and Ethics* (Selinsgrove, PA, 2011), p. 292.

9 Natalie Marie DeJonghe, *The Penalty of Patriarchy: How Misogyny Motivates Female Violence and Rebellion in Shakespeare's 'Titus Andronicus'* (Ann Arbor, MI, 2011).

10 'Kill Bill Is Feminist Statement, Says Tarantino', *Irish Examiner*, 2 October 2003.

11 Cathy Winkler, *One Night: Realities of Rape* (Walnut Creek, CA, 2002), p. 117.

12 Alexandra Heller-Nicholas, *Rape-revenge Films: A Critical Study* (Jefferson, NC, 2011).

13 Marianne Musgrove, *The Beginner's Guide to Revenge* (North Sydney, NSW, 2012).

14 Francesca Simon, *Horrid Henry's Tricky Tricks* (London, 2014).

15 M. P. Rolland, *Diary of a Mean Teacher: Mr Meany's Revenge*, ebook (2014).

16 Emily Moulton, Melissa Allen Heath, Mary Anne Prater and Tina Taylor Dyches, 'Portrayals of Bullying in Children's Picture Books and Implications for Bibliotherapy', *Reading Horizons*, LI/2 (2011), pp. 119–48; Kelly S. Flanagan et al., 'Coping with Bullying: What Answers Does Children's Literature Provide?', *School Psychology International*, XXXIV/6 (2013), pp. 691–706; Ronald L. Oliver, Terrell A. Young and Sheila M. LaSalle, 'Early Lessons in Bullying and Victimization: The Help and Hindrance of Children's Literature', *The School Counselor*, XLII/2 (1994), pp. 137–46.

17 Betsy Byars, *The Eighteenth Emergency* (London, 1974).

18 Hugh Muir, 'Rival Biographer Admits Hoax Betjeman Love Letter', *The Guardian*, 4 September 2006.

19 'Writers Write Interview with Peter James', www.peterjames.com, 9 September 2014.

20 Shannon Baker, 'Writing What You Know Is the Best Revenge', www.writersinthestormblog.com, 14 August 2014.

21 Rosemary Mahoney, 'Powerful Attractions', *New York Times*, 30 December 2007.

22 Rick Lyman, 'Martha Gellhorn, Daring Writer, Dies at 89', *New York Times*, 17 February 1998.

23 Jeffrey Meyers, 'Hemingway's Humor', *Michigan Quarterly Review*, XLIII/2 (2004), pp. 214–32.

24 Ernest Hemingway, *Across the River and Into the Trees* (New York, 1950), p. 151.

FOUR: EYES, TEETH AND JUSTICE

1 Jack M. Sasson, ed., *Civilizations of the Ancient Near East* (New York, 1995).

2 G. R. Driver and John C. Miles, *The Babylonian Laws*, 2 vols (Oxford, 1952).

3 Robert Bartlett, *Trial by Fire and Water* (Oxford, 1986).

4 The account of Queen Emma's infidelity, as told by Herbert J. Reid in *The History of Wargrave, Berks* (1885, repr. 2010), is available at 'Royal Ordeal by Fire', *David Nash Ford's Royal Berkshire History*, www.berkshirehistory.com, accessed 23 February 2017.

5 Taken from Margaret H. Kerr, Richard D. Forsyth and Michael

J. Plyley, 'Cold Water and Hot Iron: Trial by Ordeal in England', *Journal of Interdisciplinary History*, XXII/4 (1992), pp. 582–3.

6 Hunt Janin, *Medieval Justice: Cases and Laws in France, England, and Germany: 500–1500* (Jefferson, NC, 2004).

7 George Neilson, *Trial by Combat* (Glasgow, 1890), p. 53.

8 Alfred J. Horwood, ed., *Year Books of the Reign of King Edward the First*, II: *Years XXI–XXII* (London, 1873).

9 Neilson, *Trial by Combat*, p. 51.

10 Galbert of Bruges, *The Murder of Charles the Good, Count of Flanders*, ed. and trans. James Bruce Ross (New York, 1967), pp. 212–13.

11 Hans Talhoffer, *Medieval Combat: A Fifteenth-century Illustrated Manual of Swordfighting and Close-quarter Combat*, ed. and trans. Mark Rector (Barnsley, 2000).

12 Barbara Tuchman, *A Distant Mirror: The Calamitous Fourteenth Century* (New York, 1978).

13 Nigel Saul, *Richard II* (New Haven, CT, 1999), p. 74.

14 Richard W. Kaeuper, *Chivalry and Violence in Medieval Europe* (Oxford, 2001).

15 Robert Richard Tighe and James Edward Davis, *Annals of Windsor, Being a History of the Castle and Town* (London, 1858), p. 46.

16 Sara Butler, *The Language of Abuse: Marital Violence in Later Medieval England* (Leiden, 2007), p. 35.

17 Shulamith Shahar, *The Fourth Estate: A History of Women in the Middle Ages* (London, 1983, revd 2003), p. 16.

18 John F. Pound, *Poverty and Vagrancy in Tudor England* (London, 2014), p. 51.

19 David Jardine, 'Memoir of the Duke of Norfolk', *Criminal Trials*, II (London, 1847), pp. 137–8.

20 Michael L. Radelet and Traci L. Lacock. 'Do Executions Lower Homicide Rates: The Views of Leading Criminologists', *Journal of Criminal Law and Criminology*, XCIX/2 (2009), pp. 489–508; John J. Donohue and Justin Wolfers, 'Uses and Abuses of Empirical Evidence in the Death Penalty Debate', *Stanford Law Review*, LVIII/3 (2005), pp. 791–845.

21 Amy Green, 'Death Penalty Popular Among Bible Belt Christians', *Associated Press*, 19 March 2000, available at www.sullivan-county.com, accessed 23 February 2017.

22 'Death Penalty 2015: Alarming Surge in Recorded Executions Sees Highest Toll in More Than 25 Years', *Amnesty International*, 6 April 2016, www.amnesty.org.

FIVE: TRIBES AND BLOODY HONOUR

1 'Report Says 100 Dead in Yearlong Tribal Blood Feud', *Chicago Tribune*, 2 May 2000.

2 Napoleon Chagnon, 'Life Histories, Blood Revenge, and Warfare in a Tribal Population', *Science*, CCXXXIX/4843 (26 February 1988), pp. 985–92.

3 'Papua New Guinea – Tribal Fights', *Journeyman Pictures*, www.journeyman.tv, 2007.

4 Polly Wiessner, 'From Spears to M-16s: Testing the Imbalance of Power Hypothesis among the Enga', *Journal of Anthropological Research*, LXII/2 (2006), pp. 165–91.

5 Philip Alper, 'Gun-running in Papua New Guinea: From Arrows to Assault Weapons in the Southern Highlands', www.researchgate.net, January 2005.

6 Wiessner, 'From Spears to M-16s; Polly Wiessner and Nitze Pupu, 'Toward Peace: Foreign Arms and Indigenous Institutions in a Papua New Guinea Society', *Science*, CCCXXXVII/6102 (28 September 2012), pp. 1651–4.

7 Dana Facaros and Michael Pauls, *Corsica* (London, 2008).

8 'Vendetta', *Chambers's Encyclopaedia* (Philadelphia, PA, 1875), vol. IX, pp. 744–6.

9 Dorothy Carrington, *Granite Island: Portrait of Corsica* (London, 2015).

10 Thomas Barfield, 'Afghan Customary Law and Its Relationship to Formal Judicial Institutions', www.usip.org, 26 June 2003.

11 Tom Coghlan, 'Afghan Blood Feud Ends after 30 Years', *The Telegraph*, 1 June 2008; CORI Thematic Report, 'Afghanistan; Blood Feuds', February 2014, available at www.refworld.org, accessed 23 February 2017.

12 Republic of Albania Committee of Nationwide Reconciliation, 'Annual Work Analysis of Committee of Nationwide Reconciliation for 2012', www.pajtimi.com, 24 December 2012.

13 Katrin Kuntz, '"We'll Get You": An Albanian Boy's Life Ruined by Blood Feuds', *Der Spiegel*, 6 June 2014.

14 Recep Doğan, 'Different Cultural Understandings of Honor that Inspire Killing: An Inquiry into the Defendant's Perspective', *Homicide Studies*, XVIII/4 (2014), p. 372.

15 'Impunity for Domestic Violence, "Honour Killings" Cannot Continue – UN Official', www.un.org/News, 4 March 2010.

16 Davon Thacker, 'Honor Suicides', in *Encyclopedia of Women in Today's World*, ed. Mary Zeiss Stange, Carol K. Oyster and Jane E. Sloan

(Thousand Oaks, CA, 2011), vol. I, pp. 722–4; Doğan, 'Different
Cultural Understandings of Honor that Inspire Killing', pp. 363–88.

17 Austin Kennett, *Bedouin Justice: Laws and Customs among the
Egyptian Bedouin* (Cambridge, 1925); Aref Abu-Rabia, 'Family Honor
Killings: Between Custom and State Law', *Open Psychology Journal*, IV,
suppl. 1-M4 (2011), pp. 34–44.

18 Simona Weinglass, 'The Deadly War on Women that Israel Refuses to
Talk About', *Times of Israel*, 30 August 2015.

19 Ari Yashar, 'Arab Woman Murdered in "Honor Killing" by Husbands
and Brother', *Arutz Sheva*, 9 December 2014.

20 Michal Shmulovich, '15-year-old Bedouin Girl Stabbed to Death in
Suspected Honor Killing', *Times of Israel*, 26 November 2012.

21 Ilana Curiel, 'Police: Slain Bedouin Teen Likely Victim of "Honor
Killing"', *Ynetnews*, 25 February 2013.

22 Dviya Talwar and Athar Ahmad, 'Honour Crime: 11,000 Cases
Recorded in Five Years', *BBC News*, 9 July 2015; 'Combating "Honour"
Crimes in the EU', www.europarl.europa.eu, December 2015; Dietrich
Oberwittler, 'Honour Killings in Germany, 1996–2005', www.mpicc.
de, accessed 17 January 2017; Hollie McKay, 'Honor Killing in
America: DOJ Report Says Growing Problem is Hidden in Stats',
Fox News U.S., 10 November 2015.

23 Emily Dyer, *'Honour' Killings in the UK* (London, 2015), p. 18, available
at http://henryjacksonsociety.org, accessed 23 February 2017.

24 Helen Pidd, 'A "Lie" and a Rush to Her Family', *The Guardian*, 30
July 2016; 'Samia Shahid Death: "Honour Killing" Victim Strangled,
Police Say', *BBC News*, 3 August 2016.

25 'The Price of Honor', www.thepriceofhonorfilm.com, accessed 23
February 2017.

26 Julia Dahl, 'American Law Enforcement Encounters "Honor"
Violence', *CBS News*, 6 April 2012; 'Rashid v. the State: In the Supreme
Court of Georgia', www.caselaw.findlaw.com, 22 January 2013.

27 'Secretary General: Ratify the Council of Europe's Convention on
Violence Against Women', *Council of Europe*, 25 November 2013.

28 Stephen Banks, 'Killing with Courtesy: The English Duelist, 1785–
1845', *Journal of British Studies*, XLVII/3 (2008), pp. 528–58.

29 Alan Kahan, *Liberalism in Nineteenth-century Europe: The Political
Culture of Limited Suffrage* (Basingstoke, 2003), p. 160.

30 Ciaran Conliffe, 'George Robert Fitzgerald – "The Fighting
Fitzgerald"', www.headstuff.org, 13 October 2014.

31 Frederic Thrasher, *The Gang: A Study of 1,313 Gangs in Chicago*
(Chicago, IL, 1927), p. 176.

32 'Her Majesty's Inspectorate of Constabulary – Getting Organised:
    A Thematic Report on the Police Service's Response to Serious and
    Organised Crime', www.justiceinspectorates.gov.uk, April 2009;
    'National Gang Threat Assessment Issued', www.archives.fbi.gov,
    21 October 2011; 'United Nations Office on Drugs and Crime Global
    Study on Homicide 2013', www.unodc.org, March 2014, p. 15.

33 Fiona Brookman, Mike Maguire, Harriet Pierpoint and Trevor
    Bennett, *Handbook on Crime* (Cullompton, Devon, 2010).

34 James Diego Vigil, *Barrio Gangs: Street Life and Identity in Southern
    California* (Austin, TX, 2010), p. 131.

35 Anthony Petrosino, Carolyn Turpin-Petrosino, Meghan E. Hollis-
    Peel and Julia G. Lavenberg, '"Scared Straight" and Other Juvenile
    Awareness Programs for Preventing Juvenile Delinquency', *Campbell
    Systematic Reviews*, XII (2004).

36 Robyn M. O'Connor and Stephanie Waddell, 'What Works to Prevent
    Gang Involvement, Youth Violence and Crime', www.eif.org.uk, 2015.

SIX: A VERY PERSONAL GRUDGE

1 See 'The Most Satisfying Examples of People Who Got Revenge
   on a Cheating Ex', www.someecards.com, accessed 18 January 2017.

2 Beth Stebner, 'California Woman Sentenced to Life in Prison for
   Chopping Off Ex-husband's Penis, then Grinding it in Garbage
   Disposal', *New York Daily News*, 29 June 2013.

3 Paul Cockerton, 'Jilted Wife Chopped Off Husband's Penis Twice
   With Scissors after Catching Him Cheating', www.mirror.co.uk,
   13 January 2015.

4 OECD Development Centre, *Social Institutions and Gender Index 2014
   Synthesis Report*, www.oecd.org, 2014.

5 'Is Life Getting Worse for Women in Erdogan's Turkey?',
   www.bbc.co.uk, 4 March 2015.

6 Graham Smith, '"I Saved My Honour": Mother Shoots and
   Decapitates Rapist who Made her Pregnant and then Dumps his
   Head in Village Square', www.dailymail.co.uk, 6 September 2012;
   Sibel Hurtas, 'Turks Protest Prison Term for Woman who Killed
   her Rapist', www.al-monitor.com, 27 April 2015.

7 Elif Shafak, 'Rape, Abortion and the Fight for Women's Rights
   in Turkey', *The Guardian*, 9 September 2012.

8 Rohini Pande and Anju Malhotra, 'Son Preference and Daughter
   Neglect in India: What Happens to Living Girls', www.unfpa.org,
   2006.

9 'Crime in India 2015 Statistics', www.ncrb.nic.in, accessed 17 January 2017; J. Venkatesan, 'Rape Cases Double, Molestation Up 4 Times in Delhi', *The Hindu*, 13 October 2013.

10 'Leaders – Usha Narayne', www.mnsfoundation.org, accessed 18 January 2017; Raekha Prasad, '"Arrest Us All": The 200 Women Who Killed a Rapist', *The Guardian*, 16 September 2005; Randeep Ramesh, 'Women's Revenge against Rapists', *The Guardian*, 9 November 2004; Nicholas Kristof, 'In India, One Woman's Stand Says "Enough"', *New York Times*, 15 January 2006; Vaibhav Ganjapure, 'Accused Say "Justice Delivered"', *Times of India*, 11 November 2014.

11 'Woman Beheads Alleged Stalker after Attack', *NBC News*, 17 October 2008; 'Indian Rapists Get Beaten by Village Women', www.youtube. com, 31 July 2014.

12 Office for National Statistics, 'Chapter 4: Intimate Personal Violence and Partner Abuse', *Crime Statistics, Focus on Violent Crime and Sexual Offences, 2013/14* (London, 2014), available at http://webarchive. nationalarchives.gov.uk, accessed 24 February 2017; 'Stalking Statistics and Data', www.victimsofcrime.org, accessed 14 January 2017; Rosemary Purcell, Michele Pathé and Paul E. Mullen, 'The Prevalence and Nature of Stalking in the Australian Community', *Australian and New Zealand Journal of Psychiatry*, XXXVI/1 (2002), pp. 114–20.

13 Judith M. McFarlane et al., 'Stalking and Intimate Partner Femicide', *Homicide Studies*, III/4 (1999), pp. 300–316; Paul E. Mullen, Michele Pathé and Rosemary Purcell, *Stalkers and Their Victims* (Cambridge, 2000); 'Stalking Cases Soared to All-time High in '13', *Japan Times*, 20 March 2014; 'Japan's Stalking Crisis', *101 East*, www.aljazeera.com, 12 December 2014.

14 Michele T. Pathé and J. Reid Meloy, 'Commentary: Stalking by Patients – Psychiatrists' Tales of Anger, Lust and Ignorance', *Journal of the American Academy of Psychiatry and the Law*, XLI/2 (2013), pp. 200–205.

15 Isabella Merzagora Betsos and Matteo Marchesi, 'The Stalking of Lawyers: A Survey Amongst Professionals in Milan', *Journal of Forensic Sciences*, LIX/6 (2014), pp. 1592–7.

16 David V. James et al., 'Harassment and Stalking of Members of the United Kingdom Parliament: Associations and Consequences', *Journal of Forensic Psychiatry and Psychology*, XXVII/3 (2016), pp. 309–30; Susanna Every-Palmer, Justin Barry-Walsh and Michele Pathé, 'Harassment, Stalking, Threats and Attacks Targeting New Zealand Politicians: A Mental Health Issue', *Australian and New Zealand Journal of Psychiatry*, XLIX/7 (2015), pp. 634–41.

17 'Nowhere to Hide', *People*, 17 May 2003.

18 Bronwyn McKeon, Troy E. McEwan and Stefan Luebbers, '"It's Not Really Stalking If You Know the Person": Measuring Community Attitudes that Normalize, Justify and Minimise Stalking', *Psychiatry, Psychology and Law*, XXII/1 (2015), pp. 291–306; Katrina Baum, Shannan Catalano, Michael Rand and Kristina Rose, *Stalking Victimization in the United States*, Bureau of Justice Statistics Special Report (Washington, DC, 2009), available at http://victimsofcrime. org, accessed 24 February 2017.

19 'Stalking Risk Profile: International Legislation', www.stalkingriskprofile. com, January 2014; Rachel Horman, 'We Have a Stalking Law – So Why Don't the Police Use It?', *The Guardian*, 19 April 2016.

20 Harald Dreßing, Josef Bailer, Anne Anders and Christine Gallas, 'Cyberstalking in a Large Sample of Social Network Users: Prevalence, Characteristics and Impact upon Victims', *Cyberpsychology Behavior and Social Networking*, XVIII/2 (2014), pp. 61–7; Carsten Maple, Emma Short and Antony Brown, 'Cyberstalking in the United Kingdom: An Analysis of the ECHO Pilot Survey', www.beds.ac.uk, 2011.

21 Jordana N. Navarro, Catherine D. Marcum, George E. Higgins and Melissa L. Ricketts, 'Addicted to the Thrill of the Virtual Hunt: Examining the Effects of Internet Addiction on the Cyberstalking Behaviors of Juveniles', *Deviant Behavior*, XXXVII/8 (2016), pp. 1–11; Sameer Hinduja and Justin W. Patchin, *Bullying Beyond the Schoolyard: Preventing and Responding to Cyberbullying* (Thousand Oaks, CA, 2014).

22 'Distribution of Cyber Stalking Victims in 2013 by Gender', www.statista.com, 2013.

23 Emily Thomas, 'Cyber-stalking: When Looking at Other People Online Becomes a Problem', *BBC Newsbeat*, 20 April 2015.

24 'Revenge Porn Misery Merchants', *The Economist* (5 July 2014), pp. 50–51.

25 'I Was the Victim of Revenge Porn', *The Guardian Weekend*, 7 February 2015.

26 'Chrissy Chambers: I Am a Victim of Revenge Porn', *Channel 4 News*, 5 June 2015.

27 Jenny Kleeman, 'U.S. Woman Pursues Ex-boyfriend in Landmark UK Revenge-porn Action', *The Guardian*, 3 June 2015.

28 Peter W. Cooper, 'The Right to be Virtually Clothed', *Washington Law Review*, XCI (2016), pp. 817–21; 'Hundreds of Victims of Revenge Porn Seek Support from Helpline', www.gov.uk, 23 August 2015;

Sameer Hinduja, 'Revenge Porn Research, Laws and Help for Victims', http://cyberbully.org, 14 July 2016.

29 'Online Reputation in a Connected World', www.cross-tab.com, January 2010.

30 'Internet Pornography by the Numbers: A Significant Threat to Society', www.webroot.com, accessed 18 January 2017.

31 'Porn Helpline Launched for the UK's 1.2 Million Addicts', www.dailymail.co.uk, 7 July 2011.

32 Sameer Hinduja, 'Deindividuation and Internet Software Piracy', *CyberPsychology and Behavior*, XII/4 (2008), pp. 391–8.

33 Danielle Citron, *Hate Crimes in Cyberspace* (Cambridge, MA, 2014).

34 'New Demos Study Reveals Scale of Social Media Misogyny', *Demos* (26 May 2016).

35 Doug Bolton, '"King of Revenge Porn" and IsAnyoneUp Owner Hunter Moore Given Two and a Half Years in Prison', *The Independent*, 4 December 2015.

36 Jan Hoffmanmarch, 'A Girl's Nude Photo, and Altered Lives', *New York Times*, 26 March 2011.

37 Megan Maas, '8 Reasons to Rethink Teens and Sexting', *Huffington Post*, 22 September 2016.

38 Jessica Ringrose, Laura Harvey, Rosalind Gill and Sonia Livingstone, 'Teen Girls, Sexual Double Standards and "Sexting": Gendered Value in Digital Image Exchange', *Feminist Theory*, XIV/3 (2013), pp. 305–23.

39 Damien Gayle and agencies, 'Newcastle Teenager Liam Lyburd Found Guilty of Planning College Massacre', *The Guardian*, 30 July 2015.

40 'List of Rampage Killers (School Massacres)', www.en.wikipedia.org, accessed 18 January 2017.

41 Here, I draw on a number of sources: Michael Rocque, 'Exploring School Rampage Shootings: Research, Theory, and Policy', *Social Science Journal*, XLIX/3 (2012), pp. 304–13; Rebecca Bondü and Herbert Scheithauer, 'Kill One or Kill Them All? Differences Between Single and Multiple Victim School Attacks', *European Journal of Criminology*, XII/3 (2015), pp. 77–299; Juliet Schiller, 'School Shootings and Critical Pedagogy', *Educational Forum*, LXXVII/2 (2013), pp. 100–110; Katherine S. Newman, *Rampage: The Social Roots of School Shootings* (New York, 2007).

42 'Deadly Lessons: School Shooters Tell Why', *Chicago Sun-Times*, 15–16 October 2000, p. 5.

43 Sue Klebold, *A Mother's Reckoning: Living in the Aftermath of Tragedy* (New York, 2016).

44 'Deadly Lessons: School Shooters Tell Why', p. 10.
45 Harry Low, 'How Japan has Almost Eradicated Gun Crime', *BBC News*, 6 January 2017.

SEVEN: VENGEANCE IN WAR

1 C.R.N. Routh, ed., *They Saw It Happen in Europe, 1450–1600* (Oxford, 1965).
2 Alisa Rubin, '4 Questions ISIS Rebels Use to Tell Sunni from Shia', *Times of India*, 26 June 2014.
3 Patrick J. McGowan, 'African Military Coups d'état, 1956–2001: Frequency, Trends and Distribution', *Journal of Modern African Studies*, XLI/3 (2003), pp. 339–70.
4 Richard Spencer and Tom Parfitt, 'Assad Revenge Squads Stalk Aleppo Refugees', *The Times*, 30 November 2016.
5 Yaron Steinbuch, 'Eichmann Begged for Mercy Before Hanging', *New York Post*, 27 January 2016.
6 Hannah Arendt, *Eichmann in Jerusalem: A Report on the Banality of Evil* (New York, 1963), p. 277.
7 'Chile Marks 41st Anniversary of Military Coup', *Daily Mail*, 11 September 2014.
8 Gram Slattery, 'Chile Doubles Down on Prosecutions for Pinochet-era Crimes', *Reuters*, 1 November 2015.
9 Vamik D. Volkan, 'Transgenerational Transmissions and Chosen Traumas: An Aspect of Large-group Identity', *Group Analysis*, XXXIV/1 (2001), pp. 79–97.
10 Gordana Kuterovac Jagodić, 'Is War a Good or a Bad Thing? The Attitudes of Croatian, Israeli, and Palestinian Children toward War', *International Journal of Psychology*, XXXV/6 (2000), pp. 241–57.
11 'Suicide Bombers: Dignity, Despair, and the Need for Hope: An Interview with Eyad El Sarraj', *Journal of Palestine Studies*, XXXI/4 (2002), pp. 71–6.
12 Michael Croydon, 'Occupied Palestine: Humiliation and Human Rights', www.opendemocracy.net, 18 October 2012.
13 '"Price Tag" Epidemic: 788 Cases, 154 Indictments', *Ynetnews*, 18 June 2013.
14 Henri Dunant, *A Memory of Solferino* [1862] (Washington, DC, 1939, repr. Geneva, 1959), available at www.icrc.org, accessed 25 February 2017.
15 Iris Chang, *The Rape of Nanking: The Forgotten Holocaust of World War II* (New York, 2012).

16 Carmen M. Argibay, 'Sexual Slavery and the Comfort Women of World War II', *Berkeley Journal of International Law*, XXI/21 (2003), p. 375.

17 Susan Brownmiller, *Against Our Will: Men, Women and Rape* (New York, 1975), p. 52.

18 Laurence Rees, *World War II behind Closed Doors: Stalin, the Nazis and the West* (New York, 2010).

19 Andrew Roberts, 'Stalin's Army of Rapists: The Brutal War Crime that Russia and Germany Tried to Ignore', www.dailymail.co.uk, 24 October 2008.

20 Jonas E. Alexis, *Christianity and Rabbinic Judaism* (Bloomington, IN, 2011), p. 404.

21 Robert Fisk, 'Bosnia War Crimes: "The Rapes Went On Day and Night"', *The Independent*, 21 September 2015.

22 Aid Worker Security Database, 'Major Attacks on Aid Workers: Summary Statistics (2005–2015)', https://aidworkersecurity.org, 31 December 2015.

23 Philip Zimbardo: interview with Hans Sherrer, 27 August 2003, available at www.forejustice.org.

24 Philip G. Zimbardo, *The Lucifer Effect* (Oxford, 2007).

25 Paul Vallely, 'Brutalised Men Do Brutal Things', *The Independent*, 2 December 2013.

EIGHT: WORK AND REVENGE

1 Ben Richardson, 'When Office Work Turns Ugly', *BBC News*, 12 August 2004.

2 Thomas M. Tripp, Robert J. Bies and Karl Aquino, 'Poetic Justice or Petty Jealousy? The Aesthetics of Revenge', *Organizational Behavior and Human Decision Processes*, LXXXIX/1 (2002), p. 970.

3 Ian Paul, 'Ex-employee Wreaks Havoc on 100 Cars – Wirelessly', www.pcworld.com, 18 March 2010.

4 Brian Lewis, 'Disgruntled Former Employees May Use the Internet for Revenge', www.workforce.com, 10 May 2004.

5 Émile Pouget, *Le Sabotage* (Paris, 1911); 'Sabotage', www.etymonline. com, accessed 18 January 2017; Samuel Michael Bell, 'Labor Disputes, Wooden Shoes, and Italian Bread', https://jeparleamericain.com, 29 June 2012.

6 Charlotte Bronte, *Shirley and The Professor* (London, 2008), pp. 29–30.

7 Tom Broughton, 'Sabotage', www.building.co.uk, 14 January 2015.

8 'The Cross-dressing Ken Doll', www.hoaxes.org, accessed

18 January 2017.

9 Lloyd C. Harris and Emmanuel Ogbonna, 'Exploring Service
Sabotage: The Antecedents, Types and Consequences of Frontline,
Deviant, Antiservice Behaviors', *Journal of Service Research*, IV/3
(2002), pp. 163–83.

10 Lloyd C. Harris and Emmanuel Ogbonna, 'Motives for Service
Sabotage: An Empirical Study of Front-line Workers', *Service Industries
Journal*, XXXII/13 (2012), p. 2035.

11 Ibid, p. 2036.

12 'I Hate Call Centres', www.callcentrefury.blogspot.co.uk, 23 August 2011.

13 'What's It Like to Work in a Call Center?', www.forum.bodybuilding.
com, 19 August 2015.

14 Daniel P. Skarlicki, Danielle D. van Jaarsveld and David D. Walker,
'Getting Even for Customer Mistreatment: The Role of Moral Identity
in the Relationship Between Customer Interpersonal Injustice and
Employee Sabotage', *Journal of Applied Psychology*, XCVIII/6 (2008),
pp. 1335–47; Ernesto Noronha and Premilla D'Cruz, 'Organising Call
Centre Agents: Emerging Issues', *Economic and Political Weekly*, XLI/21
(2006), pp. 2115–21.

15 Stephen Fineman, *Understanding Emotion at Work* (London, 2003).

16 Ibid., p. 38.

17 Ching-Wen Yeh, 'Linking Customer Verbal Aggression and Service
Sabotage', *Journal of Service Theory and Practice*, XXV/6 (2015),
pp. 877–96.

18 Arlie Russell Hochschild, *The Managed Heart: Commercialization
of Human Feeling* (Berkeley, CA, 2003), p. 127.

19 David Sedaris, 'Standing By', *The New Yorker* (9 August 2010).

20 Regina Barreca, *Sweet Revenge: The Wicked Delights of Getting Even*
(New York, 1995), p. 114.

NINE: INSIDE POLITICAL REVENGE

1 Nancy Isenberg, *Fallen Founder: The Life of Aaron Burr* (New York,
2007), pp. 132–4.

2 David C. Hammack, *Power and Society in Greater New York*
(New York, 1982), p. 118.

3 Anne DiFabio, 'Thomas Nast Takes Down Tammany:
A Cartoonist's Crusade Against a Political Boss', www.blog.mcny.org,
24 September 2013.

4 Leigh Ann Caldwell, 'Political Vendettas "As American as Apple Pie"',
www.politicalticker.blogs.cnn.com, 12 January 2014.

5 'Nixon's Enemies List', www.enemieslist.info, accessed 18 January 2017.
6 Owen Lovejoy, *His Brother's Blood: Speeches and Writings, 1838–64*, ed. William F. Moore and Jane Ann Moore (Urbana, IL, 2004), p. 194.
7 Martijn Icks and Eric Shiraev, eds, *Character Assassination Throughout the Ages* (London, 2014), p. 1.
8 Ibid.
9 Martina Klicperová-Baker, 'A Character Assassination Attempt: The Case of Václav Havel', ibid., pp. 253–69.
10 'Character Assassination of Aung San Suu Kyi', www. archive-2. mizzima.com, 9 June 2009.
11 Annemarie S. Walter, 'Negative Campaigning in Western Europe: Similar or Different?', *Political Studies*, LXII/1 (2014), pp. 42–60.
12 Jason Smart and Eric Shiraev, 'Character Attacks and American Presidents', in *Character Assassination throughout the Ages*, ed. Icks and Shiraev, p. 217.
13 Suzanne Goldenberg, 'U.S. Election: Republicans Target Obama's Character in New Attacks', *The Guardian*, 6 October 2008.
14 Brian Beutler, 'Donald Trump is Too Chaotic to Attack Hillary Clinton Effectively', *New Republic*, 23 June 2016; Jeremy Diamond, 'Trump Escalates Attacks on Clinton's Character', *CNN*, 6 August 2016.
15 Paul S. Martin, 'Inside the Black Box of Negative Campaign Effects: Three Reasons Why Negative Campaigns Mobilize', *Political Psychology*, XXV/4 (2004), p. 546.
16 Peter A. Gregory, 'Comparing the Effectiveness of Positive and Negative Political Campaigns', *Inquiries Journal/Student Pulse*, VII/2 (2015), available at www.inquiriesjournal.com.
17 Quoted in Tom O'Malley and Clive Soley, *Regulating the Press* (London, 2000), p. 31.
18 Joy Hakim, *A History of U.S.*, 3rd edn (Oxford, 2005), p. 196.
19 Anne Chisholm and Michael Davie, *Lord Beaverbrook: A Life* (London, 1992), p. 142.
20 Ibid., p. 494.
21 David McKnight, 'Murdoch and His Influence on Australian Political Life', *The Guardian*, 7 August 2013.
22 Wendy Bacon and Chris Nash, 'Playing the Media Game: The Relative (In)Visibility of Coal Industry Interests in Media Reporting of Coal as a Climate Change Issue in Australia', *Journalism Studies*, XIII/2 (2012), pp. 243–58.
23 Janet Albrechtsen, 'Let's Be Honest About Julia's Free Gender Leg-up', *The Australian*, 28 July 2010.

24 Robert Manne, 'Why Rupert Murdoch Can't Be Stopped', www.
    themonthly.com.au, November 2013.

25 'Who Owns the Media', *European Federation of Journalists*, 6 March
    2012.

26 'Leveson Inquiry: Rupert Murdoch Appears, Day One', *The Guardian*,
    25 April 2012.

27 Jonathan Campbell, 'What the Ghostwriter Saw: "I Write, They Take
    the Credit"', *The Independent*, 31 March 2010.

28 James, Earl Waldegrave, *Memoirs from 1754 to 1758* (London, 1821),
    pp. 38, 29.

29 Denis Healey, *The Time of My Life* (London, 1990), pp. 297–8.

30 Tony Blair, *A Journey* (London, 2011), p. 616.

31 Donald T. Regan, *For the Record: From Wall Street to Washington*
    (New York, 1989).

32 Nancy Regan, *My Turn: The Memoirs of Nancy Reagan* (New York,
    1989), Chapter Ten.

33 Reported by Andrew Black, 'The Art of the Political Memoir', *BBC
    News* (15 March 2015)

EPILOGUE: NO END TO REVENGE?

1 Alice Miller, *Breaking Down the Wall of Silence: To Join the Waiting
   Child* (London, 1991), pp. 130–31.

2 Jeremy Armstrong, 'Paul Stewart: I Was Sexually Abused by Coach
   who Threatened to Kill My Family if I Told Anyone', *The Mirror*,
   27 November 2016.

BIBLIOGRAPHY

ONE: THE ROOTS OF REVENGE

Barash, David, and Judith Eve Lipton, *Payback* (Oxford, 2011)
Böhm, Tomas, and Suzanne Kaplan, *Revenge: On the Dynamics of a Frightening Urge and Its Taming* (London, 2011)
French, Peter A., *The Virtues of Vengeance* (Lawrence, KS, 2001)
Miller, William Ian, *Eye for an Eye* (Cambridge, 2005)

TWO: RELIGIOUS VOICES

Clark, Terry Ray, and Dan W. Clanton Jr, eds, *Understanding Religion and Popular Culture: Theories, Themes, Products and Practices* (London, 2012)
Kepel, Gilles, *The Revenge of God: The Resurgence of Islam, Christianity and Judaism in the Modern World* (University Park, PA, 1994)
Sivan, Emmanuel, *Radical Islam: Medieval Theology and Modern Politics* (New Haven, CT, 1990)

THREE: WRITING REVENGE

Bacon, Henry, *The Fascination of Film Violence* (New York, 2015)
Carpenter, Humphrey, *Secret Gardens: A Study of the Golden Age of Children's Literature* (London, 2012)
Tassi, Marguerite A., *Women and Revenge in Shakespeare: Gender, Genre, and Ethics* (Selinsgrove, PA, 2011)
Ward, Jenna, and Robert McMurray, *The Dark Side of Emotional Labour* (Abingdon, 2015)

FOUR: EYES, TEETH AND JUSTICE

Bartlett, Robert, *Trial by Fire and Water* (Oxford, 1986)
Barton, Charles, *Getting Even: Revenge as a Form of Justice* (Chicago, IL, 1999)
Jacoby, Susan, *Wild Justice: The Evolution of Revenge* (New York, 1983)
Kaeuper, Richard, *Chivalry and Violence in Medieval Europe* (Oxford, 2001)

FIVE: TRIBES AND BLOODY HONOUR

Fox, Robin, *The Tribal Imagination: Civilization and the Savage Mind* (Cambridge, MA, 2011)
Gill, Aisha, Carolyn Strange and Karl Roberts, eds, *'Honour' Killing and Violence: Theory, Policy and Practice* (New York, 2014)
Huff, C. Ronald, ed., *Gangs in America III* (Thousand Oaks, CA, 2001)
Onal, Ayse, *Honour Killing: Stories of Men Who Killed* (London, 2012)

SIX: A VERY PERSONAL GRUDGE

Citron, Danielle Keats, *Hate Crimes in Cyberspace* (Cambridge, MA, 2014)
Meloy, J. Reid, Lorraine Sheridan and Jens Hoffmann, eds, *Stalking, Threatening and Attacking Public Figures: A Psychological and Behavioral Analysis* (Oxford, 2008)
Nader, Kathleen, ed., *School Rampage Shootings and Other Youth Disturbances: Early Preventative Interventions* (London, 2013)
Tarrant, Shira, *The Pornography Industry: What Everyone Needs to Know* (Oxford, 2016)

SEVEN: VENGEANCE IN WAR

Arendt, Hannah, *Eichmann in Jerusalem: A Report on the Banality of Evil* (New York, 1963)
Brownmiller, Susan, *Against Our Will: Men, Women and Rape* (New York, 1975)
Chuter, David, *War Crimes: Confronting Atrocity in the Modern World* (Boulder, CO, 2003)
Zehr, Howard, *The Little Book of Restorative Justice* (New York, revd edn 2015)

EIGHT: WORK AND REVENGE

Denenberg, Richard, and Mark Braverman, *The Violence-prone Workplace: A New Approach to Dealing with Hostile, Threatening, and Uncivil Behavior* (Ithaca, NY, 2001)

Harris, Lloyd C., and Emmanuel Ogbonna, 'Service Sabotage: The Dark Side of Service Dynamics', *Business Horizons*, LII/4 (2009), pp. 325–35

Tripp, Thomas M., and Robert J. Bies, *Getting Even: The Truth About Workplace Revenge – and How to Stop It* (San Francisco, CA, 2009)

Ward, Jenna, and Robert McMurray, *The Dark Side of Emotional Labour* (Abingdon, 2015)

NINE: INSIDE POLITICAL REVENGE

Dean, Malcolm, *Democracy Under Attack: How the Media Distort Policy and Politics* (Bristol, 2013)

Dionne, E. J., Jr, *Stand Up Fight Back: Republican Toughs, Democratic Wimps and the Politics of Revenge* (New York, 2004)

Egerton, George W., ed., *Political Memoir: Essays on the Politics of Memory* (London, 1994)

Icks, Martijn, and Eric Shiraev, eds, *Character Assassination Throughout the Ages* (New York, 2014)

ACKNOWLEDGEMENTS

My thanks to Ben Hayes at Reaktion Books. His enthusiasm helped bring this book into fruition and his critical eye undoubtedly improved it.

The image on p. 115 was reproduced with kind permission of Gus Frederick, editor of Homer C. Davenport, *The Annotated Cartoons* (Silverton, OR, 2012).

INDEX